Green Lewisham
Our treasured open spaces

Candy Blackham

Published by Clink Street Publishing 2022

Copyright © 2022

First edition.

The author asserts the moral right under the Copyright, Designs and Patents Act 1988 to be identified as the author of this work.

All rights reserved. No part of this publication may be reproduced, stored in a retrieval system or transmitted, in any form or by any means without the prior consent of the author, nor be otherwise circulated in any form of binding or cover other than that with which it is published and without a similar condition being imposed on the subsequent purchaser.

978-1-914498-51-0 - paperback
978-1-914498-52-7 - ebook

Contents

	Page
Message from Damien Egan, Mayor of Lewisham	1
Introduction	2
Why are there green spaces in Lewisham?	4
Maps	8

NORTH WEST LEWISHAM — 10
Deptford, New Cross and Telegraph Hill — 10

		Page
1.	Besson Street	12
2.	Bridgehouse Meadows	14
3.	Charlotte Turner Gardens, Twinkle Park and St Nicholas Church	16
4.	Charlottenburg Park	18
5.	Deptford Park	20
6.	Deptford Memorial Gardens	22
7.	Eckington Gardens	24
8.	Evelyn Green	26
9.	Folkestone Gardens	28
10.	Fordham Park	30
11.	Friendly Gardens and the Deptford Railway Meadow	34
12.	Goldsmiths, University of London	38
13.	Hatcham Gardens	40
14.	Luxmore Gardens	42
15.	Margaret McMillan Park	44
16.	Pepys Park	46
17.	St Paul's Churchyard in Deptford	50
18.	Sayes Court Park	52
19.	Sue Godfrey Nature Park and Ferranti Park	54
20.	Surrey Canal Linear Park	56
21.	Telegraph Hill Park	60

EAST LEWISHAM — 64
The River Quaggy — 64

		Page
22.	Blackheath	65

Grove Park — 70

		Page
23.	Burnt Ash Pond	73
24.	Chinbrook Meadows	74
25.	Chinbrook Meadows Allotments and Chinbrook Community Orchard	78
26.	Grove Park Cemetery	80
27.	Grove Park Library Gardens	82
28.	Grove Park Nature Reserve	83
29.	Northbrook Park	86
30.	Sydenham Cottages Nature Reserve	88

Lee and Lee Green — 90

		Page
31.	Edith Nesbit Gardens	92
32.	Gilmore Road Triangle	94
33.	Manor House Gardens	96
34.	Manor Park	100
35.	Merchant Taylors' Almshouses	104
36.	St Margaret's Old Churchyard	106

CENTRAL LEWISHAM — 108

		Page
37.	Lewisham Park	110
38.	Lewisham Memorial Gardens	114
39.	St Mary's Churchyard	116
40.	Slagrove Place	120

Brockley and Crofton Park — 122

		Page
41.	Blythe Hill Fields	124
42.	Breakspears Mews Community Garden	126
43.	Brockley Cemetery and Ladywell Cemetery	128
44.	Brockley Station Community Garden	134
45.	Crofton Park Railway Garden	136
46.	Frendsbury Gardens	138
47.	Hilly Fields	140
48.	Ravensbourne Park Gardens	144

	Page
49. St Margaret's Square	146
50. Wickham Gardens	147

SOUTH AND SOUTH EAST LEWISHAM   148

51. Culverley Green	150
52. Bellingham Green	152
53. Durham Hill	154
54. Downham Playing Fields	156
55. Downham Woodland Walk	158
56. Forster Memorial Park	160
57. Hither Green Cemetery	162
58. Hither Green Crematorium	166
59. Hither Green Triangle Nature Reserve and Springbank Road Community Garden	168
60. Mountsfield Park	170
61. Reigate Road playground and embankment	174

THE RIVER RAVENSBOURNE AND THE RIVER POOL PARKS   176

62. Broadway Fields and Brookmill Park	180
63. Brookmill Road Nature Reserve	184
64. Confluence Park	186
65. Cornmill Gardens and Riverdale Sculpture Park	188
66. Ladywell Fields	192
67. Iona Close Orchard	196
68. Southend Pond and Peter Pan's Park	198
69. Beckenham Place Park	202
70. The Riverview Walk	208
71. Wild Cat Wilderness	212

WEST AND SOUTH WEST LEWISHAM   214

72. Baxter Field and Kirkdale Green	216
73. Eliot Bank and Tarleton Gardens	218
74. Hillcrest Estate Woodlands	220
75. Home Park	222
76. Horniman Museum Gardens	224
77. Horniman Nature Trail	228
78. Horniman's Triangle	230
79. Mayow Park	232
80. One Tree Hill	236
81. St Bartholomew's Churchyard	238
82. Southend Park	240
83. Sydenham Garden, Queensroad Nature Reserve and De Frene Market Garden	242
84. Sydenham Wells Park	246

CROYDON CANAL AND RAILWAY LINE NATURE RESERVES   250

85. New Cross Gate Cutting	252
86. Buckthorne Road Nature Reserve	254
87. Garthorne Road Nature Reserve	256
88. Devonshire Road Nature Reserve	258
89. Albion Millennium Green	260
90. Dacres Wood Nature Reserve	262

Endnotes	264
Sources	265

Lewisham's parks and green spaces are — officially — the best in London.

Lewisham Council is very proud of the wonderful opportunities they give for fun, exercise and relaxation for residents and visitors alike. Our position as number one in the *Good Parks for London* guide is the latest achievement in our efforts to become a greener borough.

And now, as the London Borough of Culture 2022, Lewisham's parks and green spaces will once again be in the spotlight — hosting community events for people of every age and background — something which many of our parks were originally designed for.

Candy Blackham, a long-time resident of the borough, has provided a beautifully illustrated and invaluable guide to around ninety green spaces. She explains how many of them were created and the fascinating history which surrounds them. Her aim, though, is to entice people to visit them both with her descriptions and her photographs.

I hope that *Green Lewisham — Our Treasured Open Spaces* will bring even more people to Lewisham's award-winning parks and green spaces. I congratulate Candy on filling an important gap in information about Lewisham and wish her every success with this book.

Damien Egan
Mayor of Lewisham

Introduction

This is a book which originated in adversity and out of curiosity. I have a lower back injury and pain is alleviated by staying active and particularly by walking. I am curious about new places and new ideas and 'I wonder what is round the corner' drives much of what I do.

When Covid-19 arrived with its restrictions I felt imprisoned. Fear hung heavily in the air in the early days of 2020 and my spirits sank ever lower until the day I realised my prison door had always stood open, I just hadn't realised it. Although there were restrictions in London I could still walk in the parks and I ventured out cautiously. My health improved and my spirits rose.

I had previously been exploring the green spaces in the Borough of Lewisham where I live, using a list of sites identified in the Inventory of The London Gardens Trust and on the website of Lewisham Borough Council.

Now I decided to write a book about all the amazing and wonderful sites which had rescued me. Libraries were closed for much of 2020 and even some of 2021 so I had the perfect excuse to collect more books which were helpfully delivered once or twice every week. Where would we have been without the marvellous delivery people and postmen?

Gradually I began to appreciate the complexity of my surroundings and to wonder about lessons for the future in Lewisham and other areas in the UK. I began to see ongoing patterns of concern for others, ongoing needs in our society, and a deep appreciation of nature and natural open spaces and the benefits they bring to people. I was surprised at how this understanding had been applied to urban developments in the past and how little knowledge is new.

But also I gained hours of enjoyment, relaxation and peace at a time which I personally found very difficult. I would like to share that enjoyment with you, my readers, and I hope the text gives a hint of history and perhaps prompts you to explore further. I hope too that the photographs share with you some of the atmosphere and pleasures of the sites and inspire you to visit.

Many people have been encouraging and helpful but I would particularly like to thank Lewisham Council for interest, help and guidance from Vincent Buchanan, and Jess Kyle and Eszter Wainwright-Deri of Conservation Lewisham; Darren Budden of Glendale; Hither Green Library and Sally Eaton in the Local History section of Lewisham Library.

Paul Browning and Julian Watson have been pillars of kind and generous support all the way through; Marshall Pinsent gave invaluable artistic and InDesign advice; Will Steeds of Elephant Books was generous with professional expertise; John King sent me a copy of his book; the Lewisham Local History Society was helpful; and Lynda Durrant was very generous and her maps are marvellous!

Grateful thanks are due to Lydia Evans at Morley College who started me on my photographic journey a few years ago and the Aperture Woolwich Photographic Society which continues my education. Members of AWPS have been supportive and enthusiastic and I would specially like to thank Stu Mayhew, Paul Parkinson, Jonathan Hood, Clive Lambert and Karin Tearle. I am incredibly grateful to everyone and would not have managed this project without their help and encouragement.

Through visiting the green spaces I met some very generous and helpful people. I would like to thank members of Friends Groups who unlocked gates, gave me tours and checked facts: Malcolm Bacchus, Michelle Ball, Jermaine Bennett, Trevor Burgess, Nick Bertrand, Carol Harris and Mike Brown, Anna-Maria Calahane MacGuinness, Clare Cowen, Rachel Mooney, Naomi Davis, Donna Davis, Paul de Sayle, Carole Destre, Maria Devereaux, Amie Dotchin, Errol Fernandes, Robert Francis, Rev Tim Goode, Steve Grindlay, Janet Hurst, Carol Kenna, Mike Keogh, Nigel Kersey, Rupert King, Martin Knight, Maggie Leharne, Chantelle Lindsay, David Lloyd, Trina Lynskey, Malvin Mitchell, Rachel Mooney, Jill Mountford, Kay Pallaris, Sandy Pepperell, Rev Jim Perry, Neil Rhind, Tony Rich, Kate Richardson, Robert Sheppard, Alona Sheridan, Lumen Silveira, Anne Slater, Robert Smith, Mark Taylor, Ernie Thomason and Nick Lee, Geoffrey Thurley, Tim Walker, Marion Watson, Bella Waugh and Ralph White. Goldsmiths press office, the Horniman Museum press office and St Margaret's Church in Lee were very helpful in giving me access to the sites.

Personal friends have been wonderful. My thanks to Marion Blair for listening, reading, and honesty; Sarah McLeery for being there; BER for unwavering friendship; Chrissie Kitchen for setting an example and robust and generous support; J-B Garrone for magical healing; Annabel Gatjen and Darren Higgins for keeping me upright and on my feet; Dr Shahryar Beheshti for expertise and endless kindness, and Liz Hills, Juliette Weaver and Charo Agero for caring.

A big 'thank you' to the members of the public who have agreed to be photographed for the book and the team at Authoright which helped me into print. In the end this has felt like a community endeavour rather than a solo effort and it has been a wonderfully rewarding journey. And finally thank you to Jeremy who walked for miles and listened to endless 'park talk'! The mistakes are my own, despite my best endeavours, and I welcome comments and suggestions.

Candy Blackham
December 2021

Below: 'Please picture me!' in Chinbrook Meadows in April

Why are there green spaces in Lewisham?

Lewisham was in the countryside of Kent two hundred years ago but looking at today's crowded streets this seems incredible. London's expansion, particularly from the 19th century onwards, was driven by the increasing population, the need for housing, the creation of new roads and new railway networks, changing political concerns, changes in land ownership and new social patterns and social needs after WWI. So why are there any green spaces left in Lewisham?

In the early 19th century Lewisham was a highly desirable area where wealthy people owned farms and lived in mansions surrounded by beautiful parks, away from the grime and crowding of inner London. The Bromley Court Hotel, once Bromley Hill and the home of Lord and Lady Farnborough from the early 1800s is a reminder of those times. The Forster family lived at Southend Hall and today's Forster Memorial Park was part of the family's farm. And Manor House Gardens in Lee was the parkland of the Manor House which was surrounded by farms watered by the River Quaggy.

As London expanded landowners realised it was more lucrative to build and sell houses than collect rent from farms and sold off or developed part of their large estates for housing. The landowners themselves often moved further into the countryside. Some philanthropic landowners sold land below market value, or made donations of land, or both, for parks and recreation grounds and some concerned individuals lobbied for green spaces to be preserved. Examples include Deptford Park which belonged to the Evelyn family, and Hilly Fields which was rescued from development by the Tyrwhitt-Drake families through determined lobbying by Octavia Hill and her supporters.

The Great North Wood once stretched from Croydon to the River Thames at Deptford. But timber was needed in vast quantities to build the Royal Navy between the 16th and the 19th centuries and large oaks in the woods were sacrificed to that purpose. Woods were also managed for industrial use, construction material, and charcoal was used for industrial ovens and in homes for cooking and heating. One Tree Hill, Sydenham Hill Woods, the Hillcrest Estate Woodlands, and some of the woods in Beckenham Place Park are a small reminder of the former vastness of the Great North Wood. They have survived mainly because of their location.

Somehow these woods hold a special atmosphere; time seems to change amongst the rugged trunks. The soughing of the wind in the branches is a different language and the sense of calm is enveloping and comforting, particularly amongst the older trees. And the real joy is to step away from the path and find another way, and another view.

The countryside disappeared under housing as the railway network expanded, but ironically it is the railway cuttings which have preserved some of that original land in small nature reserves along the tracks, including the nature reserves along the railway line over the former Croydon Canal and the Grove Park Nature Reserve.

Enclosure removed common lands from shared use and placed it in private ownership. Blackheath remains open land because it is manorial waste, but Lewisham Park was built on Lammas Land, and Sydenham Wells Park is all that remains of Sydenham Common, a vast open area in the early 19th century. The Commons Preservation Society was founded in 1865 and stopped further destruction of open land in London, and elsewhere. Today it continues as the Open Spaces Society, one of several organisations which fight to retain green spaces.

Originally cemeteries were laid out like parks and gardens and Brockley and Ladywell Cemeteries, Hither Green Cemetery and Grove Park Cemetery are today very beautiful, with mature trees and plants which attract wildlife. They were designed by people with a sense of the aesthetic, and in this tradition the Friends of St Mary's Church in Lewisham have developed a new Therapeutic Garden, and Hither Green Crematorium looks like parkland.

After WWI the Addison Act addressed the appalling living conditions in inner London areas and the London County Council, together with local councils, started building new housing estates on farmland. The design of the Bellingham Estate, the Downham Estate, and the housing estates in Grove Park was influenced by the Garden City concept proposed by Ebenezer Howard in 1898. This proposed tree-lined roads, recreation grounds, communal green spaces and other community facilities in the new housing estates to create pleasing living conditions.

Bromley Court Hotel, once the home of Lord Farnborough

Folkestone Gardens and Friendly Gardens are new parks in Lewisham, created on sites badly damaged after WWII. Contemporary housing developers may say they understand the need for green spaces for recreation and relaxation but they tend to be less generous than their predecessors. Charlottenburg Park is very attractive but it is small, and the new Confluence Park at Lewisham Station is a 'pocket park', the current jargon for a very small green space. The landscaping around the Surrey Canal Linear Park is very attractive but more like green 'architecture' than the recreation grounds or public parks of the past. Is this good enough?

Current concerns with preserving green space continue, often taking the form of local residents rescuing a derelict piece of land from housing development. In Lewisham there are currently over eighty Community Gardens; there are thirty-six allotments, all with long waiting lists; beekeepers abound; and local people have created magical community gardens at Brockley Station, Crofton Park Railway Station and in Breakspears Mews, amongst others. Sadly there has not been space to include them all.

Of course horticulture is not a static science, but subject to changes in climatic conditions, the demands of society, fashions and personal opinions. The formal and colourful bedding in public spaces which was popular in the 19th–20th century can still be found and the planting in Deptford and Lewisham Memorial Gardens is appropriate and very attractive, especially in the spring. But it is also expensive, time-consuming and environmentally challenging. Current trends are towards low-maintenance grass, drought-resistant and perennial planting schemes, as in the Horniman Museum gardens

Rewilding is currently topical but William Robinson wrote *The Wild Garden* in 1870! While the idea is interpreted in many different ways it generally includes reintroducing indigenous species of plants and trees and less mowing of verges and areas of grass. Blackheath has a new abundance of wildflowers and Beckenham Place Park has been returned to a public park with swathes of meadows instead of a tightly controlled and mown golf course.

The Ravensbourne River and its tributaries have shaped the landscape in Lewisham over centuries and an appreciation of its value and attractiveness has returned over the past generation thanks to the work of groups such as the Quaggy Waterways Action Group. There is a better understanding of how to manage a river in an urban environment and as a result the river has been opened up in parks such as Ladywell Fields, Chinbrook Meadows and along the Riverview Walk and wildlife is returning and increasing.

Caring for the parks and nature reserves is a huge undertaking. Think of your own small garden and the time, effort and expertise needed to keep it in good order. Lewisham Council and Glendale, the management company, do a tremendous job and they are greatly helped by the Friends groups in parks. Perhaps this relationship between professional and amateur gardeners has potential for development with increased opportunities for practical learning and training in horticulture?

In 1829 John Claudius Loudon, the early champion of landscape architecture, town planning and public parks, was describing the need for *Breathing Spaces in the Metropolis,* or any other city, saying that city expansion should be planned with belts of green space so that 'there [should] never be an inhabitant who would be farther than half a mile from an open airy situation, in which he was free to walk or ride, and in which he could find every mode of amusement, recreation, entertainment, and instruction'.[1]

The restrictions imposed during Covid-19 in 2020 and 2021 reminded people of the importance of green spaces, particularly for those living in urban areas. Volunteering for Community Gardens, parks and nature reserves increased and parks were often crowded. People found they wanted to feel closer to living plants, birds and the wildlife in the city, and they wanted to eat food they had grown.

This appreciation is fragile and all too easily forgotten or set aside in favour of profit, whether in London or in the new housing developments in country market towns and villages, where there may be little if any associated provision of parks or recreation grounds. If only the developers would pay heed to those who watched with sadness as their countryside disappeared under London's urban streets. In the words of John Claudius Loudon in the same article: 'It is much to be regretted, we think, that in the numerous enclosure acts which have been passed during the last fifty years, provision was not made for a public green, playground, or garden, for every village in the parishes in which such enclosures took place.'

The lesson of the past is that we live in a community and it is up to us as a community, and as individuals within our communities to do whatever is necessary to ensure our green spaces continue green and go on enhancing our living conditions in an urban environment.

River Ravensbourne in Ladywell Fields

AREAS IN LEWISHAM

North West Lewisham
Nos.1–21
pp.10–63

East Lewisham
Nos.22–36
pp.64–107

Central Lewisham
Nos.37–50
pp.108–147

South and South East Lewisham
Nos.51–61
pp.148–175

The River Ravensbourne
and the River Pool Parks
Nos.62–71
pp.176–213

West and South West Lewisham
Nos.72–84
pp.214–249

Croydon Canal and the
railway line
nature reserves
Nos.85–90
pp.250–263

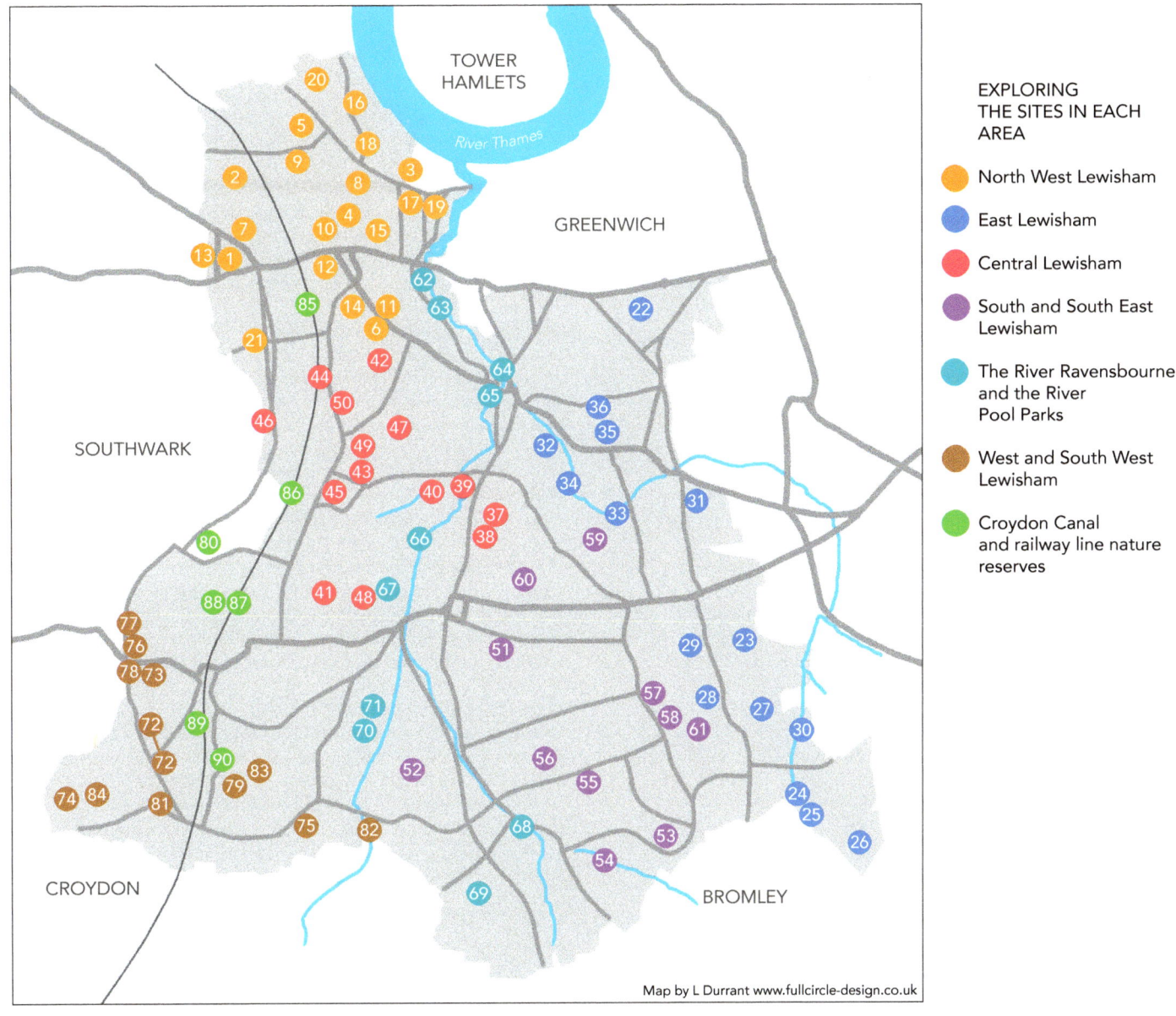

NORTH WEST LEWISHAM

Deptford, New Cross and Telegraph Hill

When the Normans arrived in England almost a thousand years ago William the Conqueror rewarded his followers with land. His brother Odo, Bishop of Bayeux, received the Manor of West Greenwich but he was very ambitious and his scheming to increase his power, perhaps under the guise of becoming Pope, led to his downfall and the manor was subsequently given to Gilbert Maminot who was the Bishop of Lisieux. Ownership of the manor changed hands many times between the aristocracy, the church and the crown until 1554 when the manor was given to Sir Thomas Pope and remained in private management or ownership from then on.

Deptford was known as Meretone or Meretun in Anglo-Saxon, meaning 'the town in the marshes' and as Depeford in the *Domesday Book*. The ford crossed the River Ravensbourne on the old Roman road between London and Dover. Historically Deptford was divided into three areas: Deptford Strond or Lower Deptford, Upper Deptford or Deptford Town, and Deptford New Town.

In the Middle Ages Deptford Strond or Lower Deptford was a small fishing village around Deptford Creek on the Thames but it was also a trading port servicing the mills on the Ravensbourne, and its shipyards built ships for the merchant trade. The status and importance of the area changed dramatically when Henry VIII established the Royal Naval Dockyard there in 1513.

Warehouses to support the Royal Navy had been based at Tower Hill, but as the Navy expanded more space was needed. In 1665 Sir Denis Gauden leased the Red House, a warehouse built of red brick close to the Dockyard in Deptford. By 1743 it was decided to move all the victualling stores to Deptford, expanding the site from 11 acres to over 35 acres by buying land from the Sayes Court Estate and with new buildings designed by James Arrow in 1783–88.

The Victualling Yard was renamed the Royal Victoria Victualling Yard after a visit by Queen Victoria in 1858 and eventually closed in 1961. The site was then redeveloped as the Pepys Housing Estate.

The dockyard closed in 1869 and from 1871–1913 the site was a foreign cattle market for the City of London; it was an army supply depot during WWI; and finally it was used for warehousing. In 1984 the government sold the site which is owned by Hutchison Property Group today. The area is known as Convoys Wharf and it is a derelict open space which is waiting for redevelopment as housing. The plans are controversial for various reasons, including the density of the proposed housing and the shortage of green space for the residents.

The East India Company established shipyards in Deptford in the 17th century close to Deptford Creek where the Company initially built its own trading ships, but the yards were sold mid-17th century as uneconomic and the shipbuilding was moved to Blackwall.

Lower Deptford's spiritual needs were serviced by the church of St Nicholas. John Evelyn of Sayes Court was a churchwarden there and some of his children were buried in the churchyard, as was Christopher Marlowe. The streets around the church were the main shopping and business areas of the time: Deptford Green, The Stowage, Flagon Row (now Rachel McMillan Street) and Hughes' Fields (Charlotte Turner Gardens). St Nicholas was the parish church until the 1730s when a larger church was needed and the church of St Paul was built in Upper Deptford.

Upper Deptford or Deptford Town was the area around Deptford Broadway and Nathan Dews tells us that in the 18th century this was a country green 'surrounded by tall, stately, luxuriant elm trees'.[2] Close by is a bridge over the River Ravensbourne which is the highest point of the tidal river, and effectively the end of Deptford Creek. From this point two main streets connected the town with Lower Deptford on the riverside, Deptford High Street (Butts Lane until 1825) and Church Street.

From the end of the 18th century Jonathan Lucas developed the area around today's St John's station for workmen employed in the Deptford Dockyards and their families and this was known as Deptford New Town. The character of the area is protected by conservation status.

New Cross was in the old Manor of Hatcham which itself was in the Manor of West Greenwich. The name was perhaps taken from New Cross House, The Cross, or The Golden Cross which was a pub at the junction of New Cross Road and Lewisham Way, where there is still a pub called the New Cross Inn. In 1613 the Trustees of the Haberdashers' Livery Company bought the estate, which was mainly farmland, to provide income for William Jones' school and almshouses in Monmouth, Wales.

As London expanded in the 19th century New Cross was well-placed to develop industries because of its good new transport links: the Grand Surrey Canal in the north linked to the north-south Croydon Canal, the line from London Bridge to Deptford opened in 1836, and extended to Greenwich in 1838, the New Cross Gate railway station opened in 1839, New Cross Station opened in 1850 on the North Kent Line, and the South London Line opened in 1866.

But London's population was also increasing and it was clear that housing would provide better income than farming. The Haberdashers' Company started building houses in the Manor of Hatcham from the 1850s, with schools and a church to service the new communities. The Church of St Catherine, on top of Telegraph Hill, is named for the Company's Patron saint. In the 20th century the Company sold the estate to private owners.

Further reading for Deptford and New Cross:

Dews, Nathan: *History of Deptford*, 1884,
    republished by Michael Wood and FamLoc, 2015
Spurgeon, Darrell: *Discover Deptford and Lewisham*, 1997,
    Greenwich Guide-Books, London
Steele, Jess: *Turning the Tide*, 1993, Deptford Forum Publishing
    Ltd, London

Above: A replica of *The Golden Hind*, originally the *Pelican*, which was commissioned by Francis Drake. The ship was built and registered in Plymouth and went on display in Deptford after the circumnavigation of 1577-80; Sir Francis was knighted on board.
Right: The original gates into the Royal Victoria Victualling Yard in Deptford with cannon bollards on the pavement

Besson St Community Garden

The Besson Street Community Garden is a community asset which was transferred to The New Cross Gate Trust and it is developed and maintained entirely by volunteers. Over the past sixteen years the Trust has invested over £250,000 in the site to realise its aims of championing causes to improve and enhance people's lives in an area with high levels of deprivation and dense housing.

Besson Street Community Garden delivers ten-week environmental studies classes, *Trees, Leaves, Birds and Bees*, to six primary schools every year, reaching 360 children. The Trust also places great emphasis on the garden for its therapeutic value in the onsite courses in mindfulness, yoga, mental health, first aid training and work with a mental wellbeing support group.

A wide variety of flowering plants, shrubs, trees and vegetables in the garden reflects the diversity of the surrounding community. The fruit trees include a black mulberry, a damson and a brown Turkey fig and there are also apples, pears and gooseberries. The bulbs are colourful in the spring and more exotic plants line the little pond later in the year. And on the pavement outside the garden is a Caucasian wingnut tree, which is a very unusual street tree.

Local people campaigned for the garden which opened to the public in 1990 with help from the Nature Conservation Section of Lewisham Council. The Community Garden is a member of the Social Farms and Gardens and a small, safe haven of peace, calm and beauty.

Access: Besson Street SE14 5AS
Opening times: 9 am to 5 pm daily
Facilities: The Trust offers a wide range of activities
Designation: Community Garden
The New Cross Gate Trust: www.nxgtrust.org.uk

Below: The vegetable garden in June

The garden and pond in summer

Bridgehouse Meadows

The New Cross Stadium, 'The Frying Pan', opened in the early 1900s as an athletics stadium but it was mainly used for greyhound racing and speedway racing.

Greyhound racing started in 1933 and was very successful until betting shops were licensed and attendances fell. Nevertheless it continued until the stadium closed. The speedway teams the New Cross Lambs, the New Cross Rangers and the New Cross Tamers raced here from 1934–63 on a track built inside the greyhound race track. And the first BriSCA Formula One Stock Car Race was held in the stadium on Friday 16 April 1954, attracting a sellout crowd of 26,000 people. But these races only continued for two years. The stadium closed in 1969 and all the buildings had been demolished by 1975.

The Millwall Football Club moved to The Den on Cold Blow Lane in 1910 and used the stadium as an additional training ground. Ideally the club would have taken over Bridgehouse Meadows but the site was awkward and development too expensive so instead the club relocated to a nearby site, north of the Meadows, in 1993.

A New Bermondsey scheme is now under discussion with significant residential and commercial development around the club's stadium, and Bridgehouse Meadows is likely to become a very important outdoor green space for future residents in the area if the scheme is realised.

The wildlife area alongside the railway line in the south west of the site is fenced off from the public to protect the birds which breed there. The rest of the site is mainly grass, with false oat-grass, cock's-foot, Yorkshire fog, red fescue and wall barley. Wildflowers line the paths in summer and are a wonderful mix of white, pinks and yellow with cow parsley, lesser burdock, mugwort, rosebay willowherb, common mallow, hawkweed oxtongue, ribwort plantain and common nettle. The scrub cover is the usual mix and there are a few scattered trees including poplars, false acacia, ash and Norway maple.

The Meadows is an isolated site, a leftover from previous activities, but the future developments seem interesting and perhaps a bright new future lies ahead.

Access: Surrey Canal Road SE14 5SU, Hornshay Street SE15 1HB, John Williams Close SE14 5XB
Opening times: Always open
Facilities: None
Designation: SINC of Borough Importance
Size: 4.54 hectares (11 acres)

Below: A variety of spear thistle
Opposite: View to the City and the new Millwall Stadium which is just visible beyond the depression in the ground

Charlotte Turner Gardens, Twinkle Park and St Nicholas Church

There has been a church on the site of St Nicholas for over a thousand years, and as you pass through the gates and inside the encircling walls of this beautiful site you feel you are stepping back in time.

Today's building is the third church on the site, dating from 1697 and restored in 1958 after bomb damage during WWII. It is a Grade II* listed building. The gate posts have curious skull and crossbone carvings which might mean plague victims were buried in the churchyard, or perhaps they are just a Momento Mori.

Just inside the main gate is a charnel house, built at the same time as the church. These buildings are also known as ossuaries and when small churchyards became too crowded, or if bones were exposed when new graves were dug, the remains were stored in the ossuary.

Gnarled old plane trees line two sides of the churchyard, with holly, some flowering shrubs, a monkey puzzle tree and two interesting varieties of fern — rustyback fern and maidenhair spleenwort.

There was an additional, walled burial ground on Wellington Street (now McMillan Street) which was consecrated in 1765. When this closed in the early 1880s it was laid out as a garden with a donation from the Kyrle Society in 1884. The site was extended to the north in 1897 and widened to the west in the 20th century. Today this is Charlotte Turner Gardens, designed as an old-fashioned village green with a wide, grassed central area, winding paths, some stately London plane trees and a Notable golden weeping willow. Charlotte Turner Park and the adjacent Twinkle Park are Green Flag sites.

Twinkle Park was created from a derelict recreation ground in 1996 after design workshops run by Greenwich Mural Workshops with local residents and schools, and fundraising by Greenwich Mural Workshops and local people.

The large pond and a metal gazebo with a movable seat separate the pond and its wildlife garden from a playground which the park shares with the primary school.

Above: St Nicholas Church gates with skull and crossbones

The pond is densely planted and the boardwalk around the pond enables children from the nearby school to use it for pond dipping.

The two parks are leased to Twinkle Park Trust from the Royal Borough of Greenwich and managed by the Trust and the Parks Department. They are included here because the sites and the St Nicholas Church, are historically part of Deptford.

Access: St Nicholas Church SE8 3DQ;
Charlotte Turner Gardens SE8 3HY and Twinkle Park
SE8 3HD
Opening times: All these sites are always open
Facilities: Seats in all the parks
Designation: Churchyard and public parks
Size: Charlotte Turner Gardens 1.17 hectares (2.9 acres),
Twinkle Park 0.17 hectares (0.4 acres)
Twinkle Park Trust: @TwinkleParkSE8

Above: The gazebo in Twinkle Park
Below: Charlotte Turner Gardens in March with a Notable golden weeping willow on the left

Charlottenburg Park

Deptford Green School in Amersham Vale was closed by Lewisham Borough Council and relocated to a modern, larger building alongside Fordham Park in 2012. The old site is now a new park overlooked by smart new housing, a joint venture between Peabody and Sherrygreen Homes which came on to the market in late 2020.

Charlottenburg Park was formally opened on 3 September 2016 by Sir Steve Bullock, the Mayor of Lewisham at the time, and after a public poll was named in honour of Lewisham's twinning arrangement with Charlottenburg near Berlin. Perhaps a rather curious town twinning?

The park is open on two sides to Amersham Grove with its rows of attractive Victorian houses. Housing in this style was characteristic of the area but has mainly disappeared as a result of either bomb damage or clearance. Look out for the plaque which says Museum next to no.38 Amersham Grove. This was once a private museum showing the collection of Captain A T Taylor, a captain in the Merchant Navy, and opened in 1890. On the north side is Edward Street or Loving Edward Lane on old maps.

The park is a delight. Children have an attractive play area, with imaginative musical planks. As the child walks on the planks they tilt, each one making a differently pitched sound, and it is even a fun toy for adults! Wooden sheep and a climbing castle provide more challenges. For older children and adults the multipurpose games arena is a generous size and equipped with floodlights.

The shrub beds are planted with shrubby Veronicas, gold-stemmed dogwood, Mexican hair grass and willow. And there are entrancing birch tree walks, wonderfully tactile columns of white under a green canopy with a winding path between the trunks. On a warm day it is quite cool under the trees, and even feels quite secretive as you follow the path through the cast iron gateways.

The contemporary design of Charlottenburg Park is imaginative and interesting and the multipurpose small green space greatly enhances the local area.

Access: Amersham Grove SE14 6LQ
Opening times: Always open
Facilities: Multipurpose ball court, children's play area, seating
Designation: Public park
Size: 0.6 hectares (1.4 acres)

Below: Looking through the birch tree grove to the new flats
Opposite: The birch tree groves, the metal gateways and the multipurpose ball court

Deptford Park

Deptford Park is a generous and spacious park with a fascinating history. In the 18th century this was hundreds of acres of market gardens which were particularly known for their onions, celery, beans, cabbages and asparagus. John Claudius Loudon, writing in 1822, tells us that 'Edmonds at Deptford is the greatest grower of asparagus and sometimes has 70 or 80 acres under this crop'.[3] And the fields were home to a small flower called the Deptford pink, identified by Thomas Johnson in the 17th century.

London was expanding rapidly in the second half of the 19th century and the London County Council (LCC) realised Deptford would soon be completely built up. So, with considerable foresight, the LCC bought land previously used as market gardens from the Evelyn Family to create Deptford Park.

The family sold the land below market value at £2,100/acre, (a total of c.£36,000), and added a further donation of money and land. Lt Col J J Sexby, Chief Officer of Parks of the LCC, laid out the park of 17 acres which opened on 7 June 1897. He felt that 'park is too grandiloquent. It is really a recreation ground of simple design, consisting principally of a central playground, surrounded by a broad walk for a promenade, with well-planted margins' and boundary railings.[4]

In his design Lt Col J J Sexby was responding to the need for public recreational spaces. The Factory Acts of 1850 shortened the working week for factory workers, creating leisure time on Saturday afternoons. There was an increasing demand for sports fields, particularly for soccer fields, and Fulham Football Club was established in 1879 as the first club in London.

Today mature London plane trees tower over the broad perimeter walk and in summer a cricket pitch is laid out on the central grassland. Deptford Folk led the Evelyn 200 campaign to plant 200 trees in Deptford Ward in Lewisham to commemorate the bicentenary of the publication of John Evelyn's *Diary*.

Working with Trees for Cities, they created a new avenue of eleven black walnut trees across the centre of the park, and there is also a small orchard on the eastern border. Heather Burrell is a metal work artist whose work

Above: Ring-necked parakeets

is widely displayed in Lewisham and her *Iridescence* stands just inside the main entrance on Evelyn Street.

This spacious park allows you to relax and expand. The trees are reassuring by their endurance and solidity and after a circuit or two round the park you will be chatting to other walkers, or stopping to admire some particularly agile skateboarder or gymnast. If you are alone there will almost certainly be ring-necked parakeets to keep you company!

Access: Grinstead Road SE8 5BN, Evelyn Street, and Scawen Road
Opening times: 8 am to sunset
Facilities: Children's playground, outdoor gym gear, sports pitches
Designation: Green Flag public park
Size: 7 hectares (17.3 acres)
Deptford Folk: www.deptfordfolk.org

The avenue of London plane trees around the perimeter of Deptford Park on a late February afternoon

Deptford Memorial Gardens

Deptford Memorial Gardens is an attractive but almost unnoticed strip of garden between the houses on Lloyd Villas and busy Lewisham Way. Planting of some kind was already in place by 1873 when there was a fourth stretch of garden alongside Lewisham College. Today's garden is only in three sections, from Breakspears Road to Upper Brockley Road.

The Borough of Deptford commissioned the War Memorial to commemorate those who died in WWI. William Richards of Brockley designed the memorial, and the figures of a soldier and a sailor were created by William Wheatley Wagstaff. Major General Sir Charles Townshend unveiled the memorial in July 1921 and the inscription reads 'Deptford's Tribute to Her Gallant Sons Who Were Faithful Unto Death 1914–1918/1939–45'.

Historic England says the formal Deptford Memorial Gardens were only laid out after WWI, and perhaps only after the Memorial was opened in 1921. The names of those who died in WWII were added later.

The gardens are attractive, with traditional seasonal planting in the flower beds, a backdrop of flowering shrubs, and some mature chestnut and lime trees. People often sit on the benches, perhaps with a book from the telephone box book exchange, and watch the world go by. The phone box on the corner of Wickham Road and Lewisham Way is a book exchange for children's books while the telephone box on the corner of nearby Tyrwhitt Road is a book exchange for adults.

And despite the constant flow of traffic on the main road this is a restful garden where, somewhat sadly, it is easy to miss the memorial and so overlook the reminder that over one million British military personnel died in WWI and WWII.

Access: Various points along Lewisham Way
Opening times: Always open
Facilities: Book exchange telephone box, seats
Designation: Public park

Above: Soldier on the War Memorial in the Deptford Memorial Gardens
Opposite: Deptford Memorial Gardens in April

Eckington Gardens

This quiet and unexpected small park is well-used by joggers, families with children and dog walkers. It has a multipurpose ball court and the mature trees offer shade in the summer. The Friends of Eckington Gardens, like other similar groups in Lewisham, are committed to ensuring their local park is valued and in good order.

Eckington Gardens is in the old Manor of Hatcham which was owned by The Worshipful Company of Haberdashers.

Hatcham House was the manor house and it was rebuilt by Joseph Hardcastle as a country mansion in the early 1770s. The house stood between today's Egmont Street and Billington Road and the Hardcastles lived there from 1788–1819. Joseph Hardcastle was a wealthy merchant who founded The London Missionary Society and supported the abolition of slavery. After his death the lease of the property reverted to the Haberdashers' Company.

When the railway arrived at New Cross Gate in 1835 the value of land increased and the Company decided it would be more profitable to lease land for speculative housing development rather than collect rent from market gardeners. The standard of building for houses, pubs and shops in the new estate was carefully stipulated and strictly controlled.

The neighbourhood shops have now disappeared, converted into housing, but the Five Bells pub which was rebuilt in 1840 is largely unchanged. The pub, and the nearby White Hart, were popular with travellers as they stood at the New Cross Toll Gate and the junction of two main roads into London — the Dover Road and the road through Peckham to Westminster. The Haberdashers' Company also built a new school, Hatcham Temple Grove School which is one of the many schools controlled by the company. Hatcham House was finally demolished in 1869, the same year that All Saints Church on New Cross Road was built.

The land for Eckington Gardens was probably part of the land around the Hatcham Manor House or in the surrounding farmland. There was considerable bomb damage here in WWII and it was only in the 1970s that the site was cleared and Eckington Gardens finally opened in 1981.

This is an interesting area to explore with attractive details on the houses, an impressively large school, a stately church and of course the quiet little park.

Access: Casella Road SE14 5QN and Monson Road SE14 5ED
Opening times: 8 am to sunset
Facilities: Children's play area, multipurpose ball court, bandstand, separate dog walking area
Designation: Public park
Size: 0.89 hectares (2 acres)
Friends of Eckington Gardens: www.facebook.com

Below: The children's playground

Eckington Gardens in April

Evelyn Green

In the mid-1800s this area was market gardens and access was from Edward Street, once known as Loving Edward Lane. Today Evelyn Green is an unusual sight in an inner-city area — a gently undulating village green in the middle of a modern housing estate with new trees around the perimeter. Just round the corner, off Clyde Street, is a small and pretty landscaped garden with no name, and another small green in front of the flats further along Staunton Street.

The multipurpose ball court is enjoyed by the local teenagers, there is a Community Centre, and as befits a village green there is a pub, the Lord Clyde, which dates from the mid-1800s and which has been under threat of demolition or conversion into flats and remains closed.

Access: Edward Street SE14 6HU and Childers Street SE8 5ST
Opening times: 8 am to sunset
Facilities: Ball court and cctv, children's play area
Designation: Public park
Size: 1.2 hectares (3 acres)

Left: The small garden off Clyde Street
Opposite: Evelyn Green with new trees and the former Lord Clyde pub

Folkestone Gardens

Folkestone Gardens was only created in the 1970s and has developed into an informal and attractive green space in an unlikely corner of Deptford.

The site lies between two railway lines, the South Eastern Railway and the former London, Brighton and South Coast Railway. Housing for railway workers used to stand between the two lines but in WWII the area was badly bombed and fifty-two people died; after that the area became derelict.

In the 19th century the Grand Surrey Canal ran from Camberwell to the Surrey Docks across the northern end of the site and on maps of 1837 Blackhorse Pond, which covered the northern end of the park, was probably a feeder reservoir for the Canal. By 1850 the pond had disappeared. The Canal finally closed in 1971 and it was filled in the following year to become Surrey Canal Road. At this point the Borough Council tackled the derelict land and created a new, small park of c.6 acres which is named after roads which existed prior to the bombing. New flats are planned opposite the park and this will change the area again, bringing more people into this small green space.

Somehow nature prevails between the roads and railway lines. The ground is undulating which makes the park seem larger and adds interest, and a large pond is home to mallards, tufted ducks, moorhens and the inevitable Canada geese. The banks are not constantly mown and so wildflowers flourish, with clover, pink stork's-bill and common mallow, white daisies, yarrow and blue speedwell brightening the grass. Lombardy poplars line the railway and there are also sycamores and willow trees.

The park has a children's play area, ball court and skate park, and the Park Cafe Hönle offers good food and drinks. This little park may be small, but it is fun because it is happy and busy with children, acrobatic skateboarders and people just sitting quietly and enjoying its openness. It is well worth visiting Folkestone Gardens.

Above: Skateboarders in Folkestone Gardens
Opposite: Enjoying the park in February

Access: Trundleys Road SE8 5JE and Rolt Street SE8 5NJ
Opening times: Always open
Facilities: Skatepark, playground, café, toilets, Quietway 1 Cycle Path runs through the park
Designation: Public park, SINC of Local Importance
Size: 2.5 hectares (6 acres)
Deptford Folk: www.deptfordfolk.org

Fordham Park

As late as 1850 Fordham Park was in open country. Maps of that date still showed a ropewalk next to Loving Edward Lane (Edward Street) and Woodpecker Lane, the main north-south lane, passed Cold Blow Farm. By 1864 some houses had been built; by 1880 housing covered the area of the park although there was still farmland, including Cold Blow Farm; but by 1898 even the farmland had gone. In the 1970s Victorian housing was demolished and Fordham Park opened in 1975.

A skateboard site by Patrick Brown was built in 1978 and sporting facilities added a little later but it seems to have been an unwelcoming site. So, in 2011–12 the park was completely renovated by Lewisham Council.

The attractive children's play area now has quirky lights, there are new footpaths and a cycle track, and new exercise facilities. The tree trail through the park has some interesting new trees such as pride of India, the Indian bean tree and the foxglove tree and their names are helpfully set into the walkway. Alongside Angus Street there are sculptured wooden totem poles and a dry garden which is a good example of cost-effective planting in a public space. The grasses will spread and there are no edges to cut!

A public memorial and bench were installed in the park in 2012 and dedicated to the fourteen young black people who died in the New Cross house fire of 18 January 1981. The Moonshot Centre on the opposite side of the park, with its colourful mosaic, was built in the wake of the tragedy and provides a Community Centre for the African and Caribbean communities in Deptford and New Cross. This spacious and attractive park is obviously enjoyed by the local community which hosts Party in the Park and other regular social events during the year.

An interesting underpass under the railway is decorated with steel cutout panels by Heather Burrell and connects Fordham Park to Margaret McMillan Park.

Fordham Park is a marvellous park for an inner-city area and attractive at all times of the year.

Right: The grass garden in June

Access: Pagnell Street, Achilles Street, Edward Street, Childeric Road
Opening times: Always open
Facilities: Play area for children under 6 years, multipurpose ball court, trim trail, table tennis tables, football pitch, Quietway 1 cycle route (Kender to the Creek), Moonshot Community Centre
Designation: Public park
Size: 3.5 hectares (9 acres)

Above: One of the children's playgrounds
Below: A totem pole near the grass and gorse gardens and flowering trees in May

Below: Off to a function in the Moonshot Community Centre!

Looking over the central grassed area to Deptford Green School and the Moonshot Community Centre

Friendly Gardens and the Deptford Railway Meadow

Upper Friendly Gardens

At the end of the 1700s Jonathan Lucas owned most of the land north of Lewisham Way. The Deptford Dockyards were very busy at the time because of the war with France and housing for dockyard workers was in short supply. So Lucas started building what became known as Deptford New Town around Albyn Street.

The value of the properties increased when the railway was built out to Deptford and Greenwich in 1836 and so larger properties were built for more affluent city workers. St John's Church and the Vicarage were built in 1855 on the site of the Lucas mansion and in 1873 St John's Station opened.

Friendly Gardens was probably created after WWII when houses were cleared because of bomb damage. Today the park is in two sections, divided by the railway line. The largest area of the park is on top of the slope and children throng here when the nearby Lucas Vale School closes in the afternoon. At other times mothers watch their small children playing or just relax with them on the grass. The lower park on Albyn Road is for dog walkers. It is surprisingly lovely, with several large lime trees, horse chestnuts and oak trees around the undulating terrain, and the flowering cherry trees are beautiful in the spring.

The Deptford Railway Meadow on top of the railway tunnel is inbetween the two sections of the park. It is closed off but there is a charming path on one side which links Lucas Street to Oscar Street. The Deptford Railway Meadow Association keeps an eye on the site to encourage wild flowers and wildlife.

Leave the bus in Lewisham High Road and wander through Friendly Park and along the path beside the Deptford Railway Meadow — you will be surprised!

The large red oak tree in upper Friendly Gardens in April

Above: Wall mural in upper Friendly Gardens

Above and below: Dogs and dog walkers in lower Friendly Gardens

Access: Friendly Street SE4 1UU, Oscar Street and Albyn Road
Opening times: 8 am to sunset
Facilities: Children's play area, seats, separate dog walking area
Designation: Public park
Size: 1.43 hectares (3.5 acres)
Friends of Friendly Gardens: www.lewishamlocal.com
Deptford Railway Meadow Association:
www.natureconservationlewisham.co.uk/2011/07/19/deptford-railway-meadow-association

Opposite: Deptford Railway Meadow and the path alongside the meadow in late April

Goldsmiths, University of London

The Royal Naval School in New Cross was designed by John Shaw Junior and built in 1843–45 as a boarding school for the sons of impecunious officers in the Royal Navy and the Royal Marines. By the late 1800s the building was too small and the school relocated to the 16th century Fairy Hall in Mottingham in 1889. In 1910 the Admiralty sold the building to the School for the Sons of Missionaries and it became Eltham College.

The original building in New Cross was bought by the Worshipful Company of Goldsmiths in 1891 who established Goldsmiths' Technical and Recreative Institute. In 1904 the Institute was merged with London University and became Goldsmiths College, or todays Goldsmiths. Over the past century the site has expanded with new buildings added to the original block or acquired in the surrounding area.

Gardens which were in front of Goldsmiths in 1912 have mainly gone but College Green, the large open field behind the buildings, has been preserved. Mature London plane trees, one a Notable tree, line the far side of the square where there are also new ornamental trees including a beautiful sweet chestnut. The inner courtyard between the buildings is calm too with a wonderfully sculptural Indian bean tree.

The gardens exude calm and students and staff are indeed fortunate to study and work in such an environment.

Access: Lewisham Way SE14 6NW
Opening times: Open during office hours; visitors can report to the main reception in Richard Hoggart Building
Designation: Public university
Size: 5.7 hectares (14 acres)
Goldsmiths: gold.ac.uk

Below: The entrance of the original building
Below right: The courtyard between the original building and the new block

The new block overlooking College Green

Hatcham Gardens

George England (1811–1878) started his working life as an engineering apprentice at the John Penn Boiler Works and Shipyards in Deptford. He made money through successful inventions and in 1839–40 he established the Hatcham Iron Works in Pomeroy Street which became the most important manufacturer of railway locomotives in London from c.1840–1865.

The company exhibited at the Great Exhibition of 1851, winning a gold medal, and George England became a director of the new Crystal Palace Company in Sydenham in 1857. The factory tested the engines on site and they were then taken by road to New Cross Station. During George England's time the Hatcham Iron Works manufactured c.250 locomotives and exported internationally, and some of the engines are still working today on the Blaenau Ffestiniog Railway in Wales!

Hatcham Lodge at 56 Kender Street, in the grounds of the engineering works, was George England's home and alongside his home he built Georgina Terrace for his employees. A strike in 1865 broke the company and George England retired shortly afterwards. Robert Fairlie, his son-in-law took over the business; part of the site was sold to John Crossley Eno for his Fruit Salt Works in 1862 and the business changed hands several times thereafter. Today Marbrey Reliance engineering works trace their roots to George England's factory.

In 1969 the remaining factory buildings were demolished for new housing and in 2010 East designed a park with a wonderful layout of silk trees, touted as a 'new benchmark for modern parks'.[5] However, the current new housing development dominates what remains of the park.

Are the beautiful trees in the original design mainly lost? Will there be a garden again one day? Will the beautiful walnut tree be given space to display its glory? And perhaps one day some information boards or imaginative sculptures could remind residents of the interesting history of their local area?

Silk tree flowers and ripening walnuts

Access: Kender Street and Pomeroy Street SE14 5BN
Opening times: 8 am to sunset
Facilities: Two play areas and a sandpit, table tennis table, chess table, dog walking area
Designation: Public park
Size: 0.46 hectares (1 acre)

The children's play area in Hatcham Gardens on Kender Street with the new flats on Pomeroy Street in the background

Luxmore Gardens

Maps published in 1870–80 show a market garden or nursery between the houses on Malpas Road and Rokeby Road. Intriguingly, Edith's Streets mentions a stream which used to flow between Malpas Road and Rokeby Road and joined the Ravensbourne at Deptford Bridge. The maps of the 1890s show a wavy line between the houses and running down today's Luxmore Gardens. New housing off nearby Vulcan Road is accessed via Nursery Close where there was a garden centre in the 20th century. Was there a market garden here with a stream in the 19th century?

Luxmore Gardens was laid out in 1958 and these days the Friends of Luxmore Gardens, who are active and energetic and care about their local green space, supplement the work by Glendale in managing the park.

Attractive murals by the artist Aspire decorate the passageway into the park from Rokeby Road and a wall at the far end of the park. The Friends have raised money for enhanced facilities including a new play area for children, a water fountain, seats and picnic tables, and they have created community events.

A grassed central area gives children space to run round and somewhere open for adults to just sit and chat. There are alders, sycamores, limes, silver birches and ash trees around the perimeters and bordering the path, and the informal borders are attractive.

Altogether it is a pleasure to visit this completely hidden green oasis.

Access: Between Malpas Road SE4 1BS and Rokeby Road SE4 1DE
Opening times: 8 am to sunset
Facilities: Children's play area, table tennis table, seats, picnic tables
Designation: Public park
Size: 0.4 hectares (1 acre)
Friends of Luxmore Gardens: www.loveluxmore.co.uk

Above: One of the murals in Luxmore Gardens by Aspire
Below: The children's play area

Luxmore Gardens in late April

Margaret McMillan Park

Margaret McMillan (1860-1931) and her sister Rachel (d.1917) were pioneers in the field of early years education for children, and they were particularly concerned for children living in underprivileged and poor areas. Margaret was an extraordinary woman who studied psychology, physiology, languages and music in Germany, was a member of the Labour Party and the Fabian Society, and fought for universal suffrage. The sisters campaigned for the provision of free school meals, good sanitary conditions in schools, clean clothes and medical attention for children. After Rachel's death Margaret founded a teacher training college in her name in Deptford, and she is still remembered in the Rachel McMillan Nursery School and Children's Centre.

The area of today's park was covered with housing at the beginning of the 20th century and it is not clear when the space was cleared for the park which opened in 1954. Originally it was a smaller open area between Watson's Street and Glenville Grove with some lawns along Douglas Way.

In 2010 the park was completely renovated and redesigned as part of Kender to the Creek, the Route 1 cycle and walking route in the North Lewisham Links programme. The work was recognised with awards including a Civic Trust Award in 2011 and winner of Best New Public Space at the London Planning Awards in 2012.

There are always children cavorting happily in the play area, people sitting on the benches and enjoying the sunshine, or sitting in the shade under the trees if it is hot, and the landscaped walk from Fordham Park to the vibrant Deptford High Street Market is a pleasure.

Margaret McMillan park is a fine and varied park in an area with few green spaces.

Access: Douglas Way SE8 4BA, Watson's Street, Glenville Grove
Opening times: Always open
Facilities: Children's play area, cycle route, seats
Designation: Public park
Size: 1.24 hectares (3 acres)

Above: Douglas Way leading to Deptford High Street
Below: A seat in the lavender

Above: The children's playground
Below: The start of Douglas Way near Fordham Park

Above: Feeding the pigeons!
Below: Summer in the park

Pepys Park

The Pepys Estate was built between 1966 and 1973 by the Greater London Council on the site of the former Royal Victoria Victualling Yard of the Royal Navy. It was named after Samuel Pepys, Secretary to the Admiralty Board in the 17th century because Pepys frequently visited the Victualling Yard in his official capacity and then would also call on his friend, John Evelyn, at nearby Sayes Court Manor.

In the 17th century the Royal Navy's victualling yard was based at Tower Hill, but property at Deptford was acquired in 1650 alongside the Royal Dockyards. Shortly afterwards the Red House was leased as a warehouse and the victualling operation was gradually transferred to Deptford as the Navy expanded. Finally, in the 1780s, the Royal Victualling Yard was substantially rebuilt as the main centre of operations to designs by James Arrow. In 1785 the Tower Hill Depot was closed down.

At its height the yard in Deptford covered 35 acres and produced rum, chocolate, lime juice and biscuits for the RN on site, supplied salted and fresh meat, and stored and supplied various other necessary dietary requirements, medical supplies and clothing. The site of the former victualling yard at Tower Hill was taken over by the Royal Mint from 1806 with a new, purpose-built building.

When the Royal Victoria Victualling Yard finally closed in 1961 some of the original buildings were retained and renovated on the new estate. The substantial entrance gates on Grove Road stand next to the porter's lodge and offices, and from here the path leads past an elegant terrace of officers' homes which overlook Aragon Gardens. Just beyond the gardens and facing the River Thames former rum warehouses have been converted into flats and a library. Behind the warehouses the stables are now flats, and behind both are tempting glimpses of private gardens.

Lower Pepys Park is a large grassy recreation ground where new oak and ash trees were planted as part of the Evelyn 200 project. Upper Pepys Park overlooks the River Thames, with views of Canary Wharf across the water. Children have an interesting playground, and a small meadow of grasses and wildflowers has replaced unused tennis courts.

But there is more to discover here.

As you walk round the Pepys Estate you will find shady and grassy squares between the low-rise new buildings, and roses over garden walls in the summer. There are beautiful old London plane trees, field and silver maples, birch trees and robinias.

This is a varied and interesting environment in which to live with generous outdoor facilities next to the River Thames, and the Pepys Estate is a fun group of 'green rooms' to explore.

Access: Grove Street SE8 3QL
Opening times: Lower and Upper Pepys Parks always open; Aragon Gardens open 8 am to sunset
Facilities: Outdoor gym gear and trim trail, multipurpose ball court in lower Pepys Park, children's playground in upper Pepys Park
Designation: Public park, wildlife area is SINC of Local Importance
Size: 3 hectares (7.4 acres)

Below: Albertine roses hanging over a wall in late May

Aragon Gardens in the Pepys Estate in May

Lower Pepys park with outdoor gym gear

Children's play area in upper Pepys park besides the Thames and looking towards Canary Wharf

St Paul's Churchyard in Deptford

One of London's finest Baroque churches stands in a small park set back from the vibrant high street market in Deptford. St Paul's Church is definitely a surprise and should not be missed.

Parliament passed an Act in 1711 and set up the Commission for Building Fifty New Churches in London to provide spiritual care for the population in areas of rapid expansion. The churches were to be similar in design and built according to specifications laid down by the Commissioners. Thomas Archer was one of the Church Commissioners and he designed St Paul's Church in Deptford in English Baroque style. It was built between 1713–30 and according to Pevsner it is 'one of the most moving 18th century churches in London: large, sombre, and virile'.[6] The church is a Grade I listed building and it still has its ossuary, situated on the eastern boundary wall.

In the 19th century the church property stretched to Crossfield Street and the unusual Rectory (demolished in 1889) was between Coffey Street and Crossfield Street. The entire site had previously been a market garden rented by Samuel Priestman from the owner Richard Wise who worked in the Deptford Dockyard. Priestman grew asparagus, gooseberries and currants, and cultivated fruit trees. Currently the area between Coffey and Crossfield Streets is a Tideway construction site for the Thames Tideway Tunnel and will be landscaped as a new public open space when the construction work is completed.

A cholera epidemic in London in 1848–49 finally overwhelmed the London burial grounds, resulting in the closure of many London graveyards for further burials. St Paul's Churchyard closed in 1858 and Deptford New Cemetery was established further away in the countryside and today is known as Brockley Cemetery.

The Metropolitan Open Spaces Acts of 1877 and 1881 enabled closed burial grounds to become public gardens and be used for recreation, even sport, but they were still consecrated grounds and so the permission of the bishop was needed.

The Open Spaces Act of 1906 gave extended powers to local councils enabling St Paul's Churchyard to open as a Public Open Space in 1913.

The Metropolitan Public Gardens Association was founded in 1882 in response to the Acts. The Association was concerned about the lack of open spaces in inner cities and seized on the closure of graveyards to create public gardens, and soon after turned its attention to protecting London squares. The Association provided funding, gardening advice, and installed seating and drinking fountains, installing a drinking fountain at St Paul's in 1914.

Today the churchyard still has its walls which separate the living from the dead. Tombstones have been moved to line the walls and the graveyard surrounding the church is mainly grass with flowering cherry trees, and a wonderful avenue of mature lime trees and London plane trees. Together with a rose garden in front of the church this is indeed a garden as originally intended.

On the east side of the churchyard, bounded by Coffey Street and Deptford Church Street, is a rectangular green space. This was the site of the Unitarian Baptist Chapel which can be clearly identified on Stanford's map of 1864. Perhaps this could also be freshly landscaped as another small park, or nature reserve, on an historically interesting site where there has been a Baptist chapel since the 17th century?

Access: Deptford High Street and Church Street
Opening times: Always open
Facilities: Seats
Designation: Churchyard, and SINC of Local Importance
Size: 1.8 hectares (4.4 acres)

St Paul's Church from the entrance on Deptford High Street

Sayes Court Park

The park takes its name from the de Say family which held the Manor of West Greenwich in the Middle Ages. Ownership of the manor was complex but it seems to have been Crown property during the reigns of James I and Charles I (1603–1649). The Browne family may have been associated with Sayes Court, which was probably the manor house, from as early as 1568; from 1611–1675 they held the manor house and land, rent-free; and in 1663 John Evelyn obtained an extended lease of 99 years.

John Evelyn married Mary Browne, the daughter of Sir Richard Browne, the English Ambassador to the French Court, and settled at Sayes Court with his wife and family in 1652. He immediately started laying out the famous gardens. What an amazing achievement it must have been. John Evelyn tells us a little about how he developed the garden in his *Diary*:

'17th January 1653: I began to set out the oval garden at Sayes Court, which was before a rude orchard, and all the rest one entire field of 100 acres, without any hedge, except the hither holly hedge joining to the bank of the mount walk. This was the beginning of all the succeeding gardens, walks, groves, enclosures, and plantations there'.

'4th March 1664: I planted the Home-field and West-field…with elms'.

'9th May 1683: I planted all the out-limits of the garden and long walks with holly, four hundred feet in length, nine feet high, and five in diameter'.[7]

Sadly the gardens did not survive his departure to the family home in Surrey in 1694. Peter the Great, who was a tenant in 1698 while he was studying ship building at the Royal Dockyards in Deptford, wreaked havoc on the house and garden. In the early 18th century the Mansion House was largely demolished and rebuilt as a workhouse, until it too was replaced in the late 1700s. In 1856 the whole site was sold to the Admiralty.

When the Dockyards closed in 1869 William John Evelyn bought back land from the Government. He wanted to create a public recreation ground in perpetuity and he approached Octavia Hill for help, but the National Trust was not yet established and the opportunity to secure much of Sayes Court was lost.

In 1886 W J Evelyn gave 1.5 acres for public use and the Kyrle Society laid out a park with a playground and a bandstand.

The garden was again redesigned in 1951. Today there are some beautiful old London plane trees, horse chestnuts, poplars, a fern–leaved beech tree, and a kowhai tree which is covered in golden flowers in May. The Sayes Court black mulberry tree is recognised as one of the Great Trees of London. It was reputedly planted by Peter the Great, but Sir Richard Browne wrote of mulberries and John Evelyn certainly planted both black and white mulberries. The elms have sadly disappeared and the long holly hedge is only a memory, like the other wonderful features of Evelyn's garden.

John Evelyn's *Fumifugium* can be read as a political text which addressed the restoration of the monarchy, but it is also of current interest because he addressed the damaging effects of dense sea-coal smoke in London, and suggested removing certain industries from then centre of the city and creating plantations of trees and scented plants.

There is an opportunity to expand the gardens and better remember John Evelyn with the development of the neighbouring Convoys Wharf site. But will the developers, a multi-national conglomerate company, want to embrace the chance to properly celebrate a remarkable man and his garden?

Access: Grove Street SE8 3LY and Sayes Court Street SE8 3LN
Opening times: 8 am to sunset
Facilities: Children's playground, seats
Designation: Public park, SINC of Local Importance
Size: 0.9 hectares (2.2 acres)

Sayes Court Park in November with the enclosed mulberry tree

Sue Godfrey Nature Park and Ferranti Park

Deptford's site on the River Thames was advantageous to industrial development because it offered easy transport of goods to other parts of the country by water. And the River Ravensbourne provided water power for the mills which powered some of the factories.

There were potteries in Deptford probably from the late 16th century until the 1960s and they initially produced domestic ware. The potteries turned to industrial ware in response to strong competition from Staffordshire in the 18th century making sugar moulds, flowerpots, chimney pots and other industrial components. There were three main businesses in the 18th century and it is the Upper Pottery which is relevant for today's nature park.

The Parry family ran the Upper Pottery of four kilns from c.1730–1891, when it was bought by James Carroll. From 1918 the pottery was taken over by Gibbs & Canning, closing in 1961 and the buildings were finally demolished in 1967. Today only one wall remains, covered in ivy and embedded with pottery shards.

The Bronze Street Nature Park was established in 1984 after robust campaigning by local residents, including Sue Godfrey. Paths were laid out and trees and shrubs planted. The park was renamed in 1994 in memory of Sue Godfrey who was killed in a road accident and in 2005 it was declared a local nature reserve.

The adjoining Ferranti Park is named after Sebastian Ferranti, an extraordinarily precocious inventor and scientist, who designed and built the world's first large electricity supply station, in Deptford. It was intended to supply most, if not all of London's electricity needs in 1891. Sadly, his talents were not adequately recognised or rewarded at that time.

Colourful wildflowers such as tansy, common mallow, sand lucerne, goat's-beard, Greek dock, silverweed and cranesbill flourish in the summer grass and attract happy butterflies. If you stand in the meadow in summer, surrounded by mature trees and summer scents, and look towards the spire of St Paul's Church through the green leaves, it is easy to imagine you are in a field in the countryside with the village church in the distance.

Sue Godfrey and her fellow campaigners would surely be pleased by this flourishing little park which is managed by the Creekside Discovery Centre.

Access: Deptford Church Street
Opening times: Always open
Facilities: Children's play area in Ferranti Park
Designation: Local Nature Reserve and
SINC of Borough Importance
Size: 0.5 hectares (1.2 acres)
Creekside Discovery Centre: www.creeksidecentre.org.uk

St Paul's Church from the Nature Park

Perennial sweetpea
Ribwort plantain
Hoary mustard with ladybird
Dandelions

Surrey Canal Linear Park

In mid-2016 an interesting park opened in Deptford. The Surrey Canal Linear Park is on the line of the former Grand Surrey Canal in a new housing development between Evelyn Street and the Pepys Estate.

The Grand Surrey Canal was an ambitious transport scheme overtaken by technological developments. It was authorised by Parliament in 1801 to support the development of trade. The canal route was planned from the Old Salt Quay pub in the commercial docks on the River Thames to Greenwich, Croydon, Epsom, and perhaps Portsmouth. The canal reached Camberwell in 1811 and Peckham in 1826, and the Croydon Canal, which joined the Grand Surrey Canal in New Cross, opened in 1809.

However, the development of the railway network from the 1830s undermined the possible success of the venture. The Croydon Canal was closed in 1836 and the Grand Surrey Canal in London was abandoned and filled in from the 1940s and finally disappeared in the 1970s.

The new park was designed and built after consultation with local people. The design retains the line of the canal in a park which can easily be maintained and which has varied play and exercise areas. The planting is clever and perennials such as sedums, species geraniums, irises, and valerian mingle with taller bushes of St John's wort, elaeagnus, and buddleia, and clipped borders of lavender, box and hebe. And of course there are grasses, particularly Mexican hair grass and *Miscanthus* varieties.

About halfway along the park some steps lead down to Rainsborough Avenue alongside a steep embankment which is divided into three sections. This was the Deptford Wharf branch railway line for transporting goods (mainly coal) between the Thames and New Cross Gate station. The line crossed the canal at Plough Bridge but closed in 1964 and the bridge was demolished in the 1980s.

In the park adults can use the outdoor gym gear while children can climb over the wooden sheep or play in the sandpits. The little squares of planting between the blocks of flats offer surprises around every corner and there is a particularly pretty grove of white birch trees. It is fun exploring this area and if you do not want to leave you could sit down in the Plough Way Cafe or The Pear Tree and enjoy tea, coffee or even lunch!

Access: Grove Street SE8 5EW or Rainsborough Avenue off Evelyn Street SE8 5RT
Opening times: Always open
Facilities: Children's play area, outdoor gym gear, seats, sand pit, cafes
Designation: Public park. The Rainsborough Avenue Embankment is a SINC of Local Importance

Below: Hardy perennials in the park

Looking down the length of the park towards Oxestalls Road

Above left and right: Small squares and high-level gardens inbetween the housing
Below left: Former railway embankment on Rainsborough Avenue

Below: Children's play are

Shops and cafes at the northern end of the Linear Park

Telegraph Hill Park

On John Rocque's map of 1746 this is Plow'd Garlick Hill. The name changed after a telegraph station was built on top of the hill in 1795 to establish rapid communication between the Admiralty in the centre of London and Deal and Dover.

The hill was in farmland and in 1884 Nathan Dews wrote of James Martin and Sons who were large dairy farmers on the slopes of the hill. Until railway trade developed (and large scale refrigeration) the market for milk was satisfied by urban and suburban producers.

The Haberdashers' Livery Company owned the Manor of Hatcham and leased land to farmers. When New Cross Gate station opened in 1839, offering quick access to central London, it was clear that housing development would offer a better return on investment than rental from farmland.

The Company first developed the flat land north of New Cross Road and then tackled the more difficult building site on the hill. The Telegraph Hill housing estate was built by the Company between 1870–1900. The layout of the estate is unchanged and externally the houses are intact, creating a uniform impression. The Company also built two schools here, Haberdashers' Aske's Hatcham Boys' School (1875) and the Haberdashers' Aske's Girls' School (1891). St Catherine's Church on top of the hill dates from 1894 and was endowed by the Company.

George Livesey, the Managing Director of the South Metropolitan Gas Company, was the driving force behind the creation of Telegraph Hill Park. He made a donation of £2,000 which was matched by the Greenwich District Board of Works and the London County Council. The Haberdashers' Company sold the land for £6,000 which was £2,000 below market value. Matched fundraising in its early days!

The site was laid out by Lt Col J J Sexby who comments that the recreation ground was tricky to lay out because of the steepness of the site. 'On the larger plot is a small ornamental lake in two sections at different levels, from which paths lead to a gravel promenade at a high elevation, in the centre of which is a bandstand.

This plot also contains a handsome drinking fountain, the gift of Mr Livesey. The smaller plot, which crowns the summit of the hill, is more level, and upon this lawn tennis and children's games are practicable'.[8] The new park opened in 1895.

By the 1990s the park was in a dreadful state with the railings and gates gone, the original ponds filled in, no play equipment and derelict toilets. The Telegraph Hill Society started a campaign to rescue the park in 1993, set up the Friends of Telegraph Hill Park, and with funding from the Heritage Lottery Fund and Lewisham Council the restored park was opened in 2005.

Surely Lt Col J J Sexby would be pleased to see the park today? His recommended outlook, towards Knockholt Beeches in the south has gone, but the views over London are glorious on a warm summer evening. Kitto Road still divides the park, a tennis court has replaced the semaphore station and recreational facilities are good; only the bandstand and drinking fountain have gone.

The real glory are the mature trees including stately London plane trees, hornbeams, lime trees, a maidenhair tree, Indian bean tree, redwood and hornbeams and beech trees which glow in the soft autumn light.

Access: Kitto Road SE14 5TW, Drakefell Road SE14 5SH and entrances on Pepys, Erlanger and Arbuthnot Roads
Opening times: 8 am to sunset (check the website)
Facilities: Tennis courts, children's play area, skateboard park, toilets (restricted opening), seats. The Hill Station Cafe is situated between the two sections of park in Kitto Road.
Designation: Green Flag public park, SINC of Local Importance
Size: 4 hectares (10 acres)
Friends of Telegraph Hill Park: www.thehill.org.uk/park

A sunny evening in upper Telegraph Hill park in November

Hornbeams, beach and ornamental fruit trees in lower Telegraph Hill park in late November

Part of the children's play area in lower Telegraph Hill park in late November

EAST LEWISHAM

In the East of Lewisham we find Blackheath and the former Manor of Lee which includes Grove Park, Lee Green and Lee itself. And the feature of this part of Lewisham is the River Quaggy which flows through several of the parks and nature reserves.

Further reading:

Butts, R: *Butts' Historical Guide to Lewisham, Ladywell, Lee, Blackheath and Eltham*, 1878, reprinted by Amazon UK
Hart, F H: *History of Lee and its Neighbourhood*, 1882, Leopold Classic Library, reprinted by Amazon UK
Rhind, Neil: *The Heath*, 2002, Burlington Press, (Cambridge) Ltd

The River Quaggy

The River Quaggy is 17kms (10.5 miles) in length from its source in Locksbottom to the confluence with the River Ravensbourne in the newly created Confluence Park in the centre of Lewisham. Add to this thirteen named tributaries and you have a very complicated little river. Not all of the Quaggy is visible today and perhaps even the course has been changed over time to accommodate housing and roads.

The river used to be called Lee Water or Quagga and it was thought this referred to its marshy surrounds. It was only in the mid-1800s that it became the Quaggy.

In eastern Lewisham we can see the river in Confluence Park near Lewisham Station where the Quaggy joins the Ravensbourne. It is culverted until Manor Park and then appears again in Manor House Gardens. We can peer over the bridge in the middle of Lee Green, but the next sections of the Quaggy — in Weigall Road Sports Ground, Cator Park, and Sutcliffe Park — are in the London Borough of Greenwich. The Quaggy flows alongside Sydenham Cottages Nature Reserve and is out in the open air in Chinbrook Meadows. After this the river is again outside the Borough of Lewisham, with tributaries in Sundridge Park and Petts Wood, and finally Crofton Heath and Ninehams Woods, the source of the river.

The river has a history of flooding. On 11 April 1878 'Lee and Lewisham were visited with a disastrous inundation' which flooded houses and destroyed bridges and businesses. And the cause of the destruction, said F H Hart, was the 'many hard roads and asphalte paths [so that] the whole of the storm water rushes in a torrent into the valley of the Quaggy and Ravensbourne'.[9]

If you would like to make a serious study of the river please refer to Ken White's book and Paul Browning's website.

Further reading:

Browning, Paul: www.runner500.wordpress.com
White, Ken: *Quaggy River and its catchment area*, 1999, republished by Quaggy Waterways Action Group: www.qwag.org.uk

Blackheath

Blackheath is a vast and open acid grassland with various indigenous plants appropriate to this soil type. The name, Blackheath, is probably derived from Bleak Heath rather than the colour of the soil. It is Manorial waste, which is to say it is open ground which is not built on and not used for horticultural or agricultural purposes. And it is important, with a long history of notable events because of its proximity to the centre of London.

The Romans built Watling Street (today's A2) from Dover to London across the Heath and it was subsequently the gathering place for rebellions and ceremonies. The Danish invaders camped here in 1011; the followers of Wat Tyler gathered on the Heath during the Peasants' Revolt in 1381; the Jack Cade rebels opposing taxation camped on the Heath in 1450; and the Cornishmen rebelled against taxation in 1497 and many were killed in a fight on the Heath.

Over the centuries the Heath was excavated for gravel, sand, and chalk and activity increased from the 17th century as London started to expand. Marr's Ravine lay between the Hare and Billet Road and Goffers Road, Crown Pits and Washerwomen's Pits were near All Saints' Church, but the pits were mainly filled in after WWII. Blackheath Vale, now built up with housing was another of the pits. Eliot Pit, alongside St Austell Road in the south west corner of the Heath, is today filled with trees and undergrowth and looks like a woodland hillside, rather than a gravel pit. Vanbrugh Pits, GLA 63, on the north east corner of the Heath, give an idea of the original appearance of the pits and also exposes the Blackheath pebbles. At the right time of year the depression is filled with bright yellow gorse and broom. There used to be seven ponds on Blackheath but only four survive: the Hare and Billet Pond, Mounts Pond, the Princess of Wales Pond and Folly Pond which has recently also been called Long Pond.

The major landowner on the Heath was the Legge family (later the Earls of Dartmouth) which enclosed part of the Heath in the west and south east and sanctioned the building of houses.

Residential development only really started in the 1800s; before that the village consisted of two public houses, The Three Tuns and The Crown, a few cottages and a well at the

Above: The Rangers House of 1723 houses the Julius Wernher Art

bottom of the hill near today's railway line which runs along the line of the Kidbrooke (a tributary of the Quaggy). In the 1800s building started to encroach on the common land and, similar to other areas in Lewisham, the arrival of the railway in the 1849 stimulated rapid expansion of smaller homes and terraces of houses around the perimeters of the Heath.

Fairs have always been a regular feature of the Heath, and the wide expanses of grassland are ideal for sport. The Royal Blackheath Golf Club was established on the Heath in 1766, the first golf club outside Scotland, and since 1923 the club has been based in Eltham. Goffers Road remembers the golfers. Cricket was played on the Heath from the 18th century and by 1890 the LCC was maintaining thirty-six pitches on the Heath. The Blackheath Football Club was founded in 1862 by some old boys of the Blackheath Proprietary School and today shares a base with the Blackheath Cricket Club in Rectory Fields in Charlton. (The oldest clubs playing by Rugby Union rules are known as Football Clubs, which is somewhat confusing.) And the Heath and Greenwich Park are the starting points for the London Marathon.

'The legal status of the Heath is complex. North of the A2 it is owned by the Crown and managed by Greenwich, and to the South by the Earl of Dartmouth and managed by Lewisham. But all the Heath is held in trust for public benefit under the Metropolitan Commons Amendment Act [of 1869]'[10] which gave rise to the Metropolitan Commons (Supplemental) Act of 1871 and the Blackheath Scheme which prevented the planting of trees on the Heath to maintain its open character. The Commons Preservation Society was founded in 1865 and was the driving force behind the Act.

Access: All the roads around Blackheath are open to the heath
Opening times: Always open
Facilities: Seats
Designation: Green Flag public open space,
SINC of Metropolitan Importance
Size: 112 hectares (275 acres)
The Blackheath Society: www.blackheath.org

Above: Kite-flying day on the Heath
Below: Sunset at The Point

Below: Paragliding on the Heath

The Heath in Summer, looking towards Blackheath Village over the Hare and Billet Pond with the pub on the right

The Princess of Wales pond in February

The Folly Pond in June with yellow flag irises

Grove Park

Grove Park was only known as such from the late 1800s; before that the area was the southern part of the Manor of Lee, in Kent. This was countryside and covered in woods but by the 18th century most of the trees had been cut down to produce charcoal for burning in London. Today only Elmstead Wood and Marvels Wood remain and the past is remembered in the names of local roads such as Burnt Ash Lane, Ashwater Road and Ashdale Road, amongst others.

In 1792 Sir Francis Baring bought the Manor of Lee, making him the major landowner in the area together with the Crown Estate whose lands were managed by the Commissioners of Woods and Forests. The third major landowner was the Worshipful Company of Mercers, one of the Great Twelve City Livery Companies.

Once the land had been cleared it could be farmed and from 1727 Burnt Ash Farm covered most of the area. When Matthew Butler died, the second generation farmer at Burnt Ash Farm, the farm was broken up to create the smaller holdings of Grove Farm, Claypit Farm and College Farm. The soil from Claypit Farm was made into sugar loaf moulds in the pottery kilns in Greenwich, perhaps even in the pottery kilns on the site of today's Sue Godfrey Nature Reserve (no.19)? There were also market gardens supplying fruit and vegetables to London.

Hope Farm Dairy started up in the 1890s in Marvels Lane, and farming continued into the 20th century. A dairy farm at the north end of Baring Road eventually became a distribution depot for Unigate, only closing down in 2000. Melrose Farm was started in the early 1900s as a market garden behind the new villas on Burnt Ash Hill; and a piggery and poultry farm which had been set up during WWII was only replaced by housing on the Marbrook Estate in the 1960s.

Urban development started with the arrival of the railways. The South Eastern Railway line from Charing Cross to Tonbridge and the Kent coast opened in the 1860s; Grove Park Station opened in 1871, probably financed by John Pound and Edgar Drewett; and a new line to Bromley North opened in 1878.

The trains offered quick and affordable travel from offices in London to custom-built new villas in the countryside.

Above: The Baring Hall Hotel designed by Ernest Newton

Fortuitously, the clay in the area was also suitable for brickmaking. John Pound owned two brickworks here, managed by Edgar Drewett. But Pound was also a builder and in 1873 he bought Grove Farm with the aim of building houses. He worked closely with the landowner Thomas Baring, Lord Northbrook, and to gain his approval to build a pub he engaged Ernest Newton who was a distinguished but largely forgotten architect. Newton designed several of the new villas as well as the Baring Hall Hotel which opened in 1882.

Another significant developer in the area was Silas Honeywell. By 1885 there were more than fifty new villas and for the first time the area was known as Grove Park. John Pound built Saville House for himself in 2 acres of grounds on Baring Road. The Wates family started developing their company here as well. The new homes were very substantial, custom-built for the wealthy, but sadly none of these country villas remain today. An expanding community needed a church and in 1886 Lord Northbrook laid the foundation stone of St Augustine's Church. A century later Desmond Tutu, later Archbishop of Cape Town in South Africa, would live in Grove Park and be closely involved with the Church.

Grove Park Hospital was built as a workhouse in 1902 on the site of Spicers Meadow by the Greenwich Board of Guardians. It was not popular, often referred to as a 'pauper's palace' in the press. John King tells us 'It had a short history as a workhouse for Greenwich from 1903 until 1914. During WWI it was the barracks of the Army Service Corps Motor Transport section, functioning as a mobilisation and training centre. From 1926 it was the main TB hospital for South London, and then became a centre for general thoracic surgery in the 1950s. Finally in the 1990s it was a centre and home for people with learning difficulties. It was largely vacated by the NHS in 1993. Much of the complex was subsequently demolished but the attractive frontage was retained and locally listed, while most of the remaining land was developed as modest mixed housing'.

More affordable housing developed gradually in Grove Park in the 20th century. After WWI and in response to the Addison Act of 1919, there was pressure to rehouse people living in slum areas in inner London, particularly Deptford. Lewisham Council built the Grove Park Estate 1920s, and the Chinbrook Estate and Marbrook Estate followed in the 1960s. WWI also saw a change a social behaviour, with people less willing to be 'in service' and the maintenance of large mansions in extensive grounds became too expensive to sustain.

The southern part of Lee changed from countryside with some farmhouses and workers cottages in the late 19th century to the urban spread of Grove Park today. The Grove Park Heritage Trail is an interesting little map and guide to the area. The local people campaign actively to preserve the historical heritage of Grove Park and to improve leisure and recreational facilities for local residents. Perhaps the most fascinating idea is to create a new linear park, The Railway Children Urban National Park, which would stretch from St Mildred's Road down to Elmstead Woods.

Further reading:

Browning, Paul: www.runner500.wordpress.com
Hart, F H: *History of Lee and its Neighbourhood*, 1882; republished by Leopold Classic Library
King, John: *Grove Park Revisited*, 2011
The Baring Trust: www.thebaringtrust.com

Right: The former Workhouse and Grove Park Hospital and now a residential development

St Augustine's Church on Baring Road

Burnt Ash Pond

Burnt Ash Pond hides away, an oasis of calm in the middle of the Melrose housing estate which was built in 1983-84 near the busy Burnt Ash Hill road.

Why is there a pond here? In the mid-1800s Melrose Farm, Horn Park Farm and College Farm are shown on the OS Map of the area. By 1894–96 villas were built on part of College Farm and a pond is shown in the back garden of one of the villas. So perhaps Burnt Ash Pond was originally a farm pond, perhaps on College Farm, and used for watering cattle as this was a mainly dairy farm.

The pond is rich in plant and aquatic life and surrounded by mature trees including oak and crack willow. There is even a single black mulberry tree which is thought to date from the 19th century when the pond was in the back garden of a villa on Burnt Ash Hill. While mulberry trees have been planted in London since Roman times they became particularly plentiful in the 17th century when King James I wanted to create a silk industry in England to rival that of France.

Aquatic plants include yellow iris, varieties of willowherb, water plantain and water crowfoot, and toads, frogs and newts breed happily in the pond, together with beetles and spiders. Understandably, the site is popular with local schools for pond dipping.

Access: Melrose Close SE12 0AL or from the signposted footpath on Burnt Ash Hill
Opening times: Open on the first Sunday in the month, between April and November
Facilities: None
Designation: SINC of Borough Importance
Size: 0.13 hectares (0.3 acres

Chinbrook Meadows

Chinbrook Meadows in December

Chinbrook Meadows is a large and wonderfully varied green space with a river, trees, woodland, hidden fields and an orchard. It is enjoyed by visitors and local residents and nurtured by the Friends of Chinbrook Meadows.

In the 1920s The Lewisham Council bought 43 acres of farmland to build the Grove Park Estate. They set aside 8 acres for a recreation area, and another 1.5 acres for allotments. In 1929 Chinbrook Meadows was declared a public park.

The Worshipful Company of Mercers owned Chinbrook Meadows and in the 1930s they were under pressure to sell to Wates Builders for more housing. (Wates had already built the Northbrook Estate in the area). The local residents objected and after tricky negotiations Lewisham Council bought a further 23 acres and the park was relandscaped to include more sports facilities. The enlarged Chinbrook Meadows reopened in 1937.

Recreational facilities are good. Sports pitches for soccer and cricket are marked out on the two central grassy areas and there is also a ball court, tennis courts and outdoor gym gear for adults.

Children play in a specially fenced and protected play area in the main park, and in a small area alongside the cafe. In the winter the wide, paved perimeter track is dry and popular with both walkers and runners and a circular route in the park offers 0.8 miles or 2,000 steps. The Green Chain Walk and the Capital Ring Walk are two interesting long-distance paths in London which cross the park. Of course organised or strenuous exercise is not compulsory — one can just stroll in Chinbrook Meadows!

Perhaps the best reason for visiting is the River Quaggy which used to be confined in concrete channels, fenced off from the public and a barrier in the middle of the park. An imaginative restoration project in 2002 restored the river to its natural, meandering course, creating pools and wetlands. This allows the water to spill over into a small flood plain in the park and thereby slows the rush of water in heavy rain and prevents more severe flooding downstream.

The riverside is home to wetland plants including water plantain, fool's watercress, willowherb, flag iris, lesser celandine, and pendulous sedge, while alders and

The River Quaggy in its flood plain in Chinbrook Meadows in winter, with the playing fields beyond

willows line the river banks, hanging gracefully over the water. Spiders, damsel flies and dragonflies breed happily here and there is an increasing bird population, including brilliant blue kingfishers. Today the river gives untold pleasure to children playing Pooh sticks and water-loving dogs. The QWAG campaigned relentlessly for river restoration and has been richly rewarded.

Add to this the woodland of oak, sycamore and holly on the embankment alongside the railway and up the hill, the stately avenue of Lombardy poplar trees and several mature and spreading pedunculate oak trees and you have a small piece of countryside.

A new fruit orchard which was planted in 2013 hides away on the far side of the railway tunnel alongside an open green field where dogs happily chase balls. At the bottom of the field the Border Ditch runs alongside the railway embankment to join the Quaggy. This ditch and bank was the boundary of the mediaeval parish of Lee and can also be seen behind the houses on Oakbrook Close BR1 5DG.

Chinbrook Meadows is just pure delight! This is a space in which to unwind and savour nature, a space in which to slow down and be enriched at all times of the year.

Access: Amblecote Road SE12 9TR
Opening times: 8 am to sunset
Facilities: Cafe, toilets, ball court, cycle route, football pitch, cricket pitch, tennis courts and table tennis table, outdoor gym gear, play area for both younger and older children
Designation: SINC of Borough Importance
Size: 11 hectares (27 acres)
Friends of Chinbrook Meadows: www.chinbrookmeadows.wordpress.com

Below: The avenue of poplar trees in the winter sunshine

The meadow beyond the railway and the confluence of the Border Ditch with the River Quaggy in April

Chinbrook Meadows Allotments and Chinbrook Community Orchard

The allotments and community orchard are on top of the hill and separate from Chinbrook Meadows and its little orchard.

The Chinbrook Community Orchard was first planted in 1991 and has over fifty traditional (mostly Kentish) varieties of fruit trees, including apples, plums and a quince tree, and it is delight in the spring with its carpet of daffodils. It has been described as 'one the most diverse and traditional orchards in the borough and a Habitat of Principal Importance'.[11]

On the site there are two ponds filled with pond life, log piles to keep bugs safe, and flowering grassland with grass vetchling and agrimony for bees, birds, and butterflies. Together with the plants and flowers in the individual allotments it creates a small nature reserve.

Allotments are well-tended and there is keen competition for the best results. The Green Chain Walk runs along the south side of the site and allows walkers to peer through the hedges and see the gardeners hard at work at all times of the day.

The site is closed to the general public, but if there is ever an Open Day do visit to meet the gardeners and enjoy the views — you will not be disappointed!

Access: Marvels Lane SE12 9PU
Opening times: Closed to the general public;
check website for Open Days
Designation: SINC of Borough Importance
Size: 2 hectares (5 acres)
Chinbrook Meadows Horticultural Society and Community Orchard: www.facebook.com/Chinbrook-Meadows-Horticultural-Society-and-Community-Orchard

Apple trees flowering in the orchard in spring

Above: Gretchen's cheerful corner on the allotments
Below: The orchard in early spring

Above: Michele on his allotment
Below: Bee hives

Grove Park Cemetery

St Paul's Churchyard in Deptford closed for further burials in 1858 because it was full and so the Deptford Burial Board bought land for a new cemetery in Brockley. But by 1930 even Brockley Cemetery was nearly full and the Burial Board again bought undeveloped land, this time in Grove Park.

H Morley Lawson, the Borough Surveyor, designed the layout of the cemetery with appropriate amenities which included a lodge, office, chapel, drinking fountain, toilets and a nursery, and the second Deptford New Cemetery opened in 1935. Today it is known as Grove Park Cemetery.

The original cemetery lies on top of the hill, with terraces and paths curving around the hillside, and in 2003 it was listed as a Grade II site of special historic interest. The area under the brow of the hill is particularly attractive: seats invite visitors to sit quietly, looking towards Marvels Wood and Elmstead Wood in the east, or down the hill over the hidden railway line to Sundridge Park and beyond. The site has been extended on the level ground below the hill and this extension, where the graves are in more usual straight lines, is not listed.

The War Graves Commission cares for 56 graves in the cemetery, some in a formal memorial garden and others placed with family members. A large memorial wall at the nearby mass grave lists civilians killed in Deptford during WWII.

The cemetery is not covered in dense woodland, like Brockley Cemetery, but there are sufficient large trees (oaks, sycamores, cypress, ash, willow, black poplars) in the original cemetery to create a natural setting.

While this is in many ways a joyful site, with colourfully decorated graves and far views, the beauty does not hide the inherent sadness.

Access: Marvels Lane SE12 9PU
Opening times: 10 am to 4 pm daily but closed for burials; check the Lewisham Borough Council website for closure times
Facilities: Toilets
Designation: SINC of Borough Importance
Size: 9.32 hectares (23 acres)

Below: In the old cemetery

Terracing and curving paths on the side of the hill in the original cemetery

Grove Park Library Gardens

The Grove Park Library Gardens is a play area for very young children with plenty of grass for running around. This sloping, grassy site is an opportunity to create a more appealing park and varied community centre for the area and the Grove Park Neighbourhood Development Plan 2019 offers detailed proposals.

Access: Somertrees Avenue, SE12 0BX
Opening times: 8 am to sunset
Facilities: Children's play area for under-5s
Designation: Metropolitan Open Land.
Size: 0.8 hectares (1.98 acres)

Grove Park Nature Reserve

Grove Park Nature Reserve is hidden between the houses on a busy main road and the railway line and it is just delightful despite an unpromising location.

The line from Charing Cross down to Tonbridge opened in 1865 and the railway company owned most of the wide piece of land along the line between St Mildred's Road and Grove Park Station as part of the marshalling yard. Remarkably not all this land was covered with housing and some of it was previously tennis courts, allotments or private gardens behind the villas on Baring Road. In 1984 Grove Park Nature Reserve was designated and in 1987 Lewisham Council bought the freehold of the land.

A metalled path called The Railway Children Walk leads from Baring Road to the site. The path is named after Edith Nesbit's book because she once lived in The Gables, a large house (now demolished) on Baring Road.

The Grove Park Nature Reserve is a very important site, both in ecological terms and because it is part of a campaign to create the Railway Children Urban National Park which would stretch from St Mildred's Road to Elmstead Wood. The vision is a linear green nature reserve of c.4.5kms on the land above the railway line.

The main part of the reserve is woodlands of pedunculate and sessile oaks, ash, some hornbeam and an undergrowth of hawthorn, blackthorn, brambles and ivy. There are even fruiting plum trees remaining from the private gardens.

In the spring you can find bluebells, dog violets, lesser celandine, cow parsley and the three-cornered leek. A tiny stream feeds a small pond and there are delightful clearings amongst the trees.

On the western side is an open, sunny slope untouched since the railway was built and the only site of chalk grassland in Lewisham. In summer the grass is bright with wildflowers such as knapweed, common vetch, agrimony, and creeping jenny and butterflies fluttering busily.

The woods feel happy — perhaps the trees remember the pleasure people felt when they played tennis here or enjoyed their allotments.

Access: The Railway Children Walk off Baring Road SE12 0UW
Opening times: Always open
Facilities: None
Designation: Local Nature Reserve, SINC of Borough Importance
Size: 6.45 hectares (16 acres)
Friends of Grove Park Nature Reserve:
www.groveparknaturereserve.wordpress.com

Below: A marbled white butterfly in the meadow

The grassy bank overlooking the railway line in April

A path through the woods in April

Northbrook Park

The Baring family owned the Manor of Lee and in 1898 Lord Northbrook offered Ten Acre Field to the London County Council for public use and to commemorate Queen Victoria's Diamond Jubilee. This became Northbrook Park and a sundial in the park remembers Lord Northbrook's gift. The park was designed by Lt Col J J Sexby, the Chief Officer of Parks of the LCC, and opened on 14 March 1903.

Northbrook Park is well-equipped and offers the local community of all ages various forms of exercise. The grassed central area of the park is closed off and inside the iron railings there are football pitches, a trim trail, an outdoor gym and a children's playground with a splashpad.

Outside the railings the paved path of 0.3 miles, or 500 steps, is used by joggers and walkers, and at the far end of the park there is a multipurpose ball court. The Northbrook Community Group is strongly supportive of its local park in various ways including raising money for new facilities.

The wildlife area in the south west corner is used regularly by a local school for Forest School learning, teaching children a wide variety of skills about nature and about themselves. Grassland, a small wetland area, and bird boxes on the trees make this an interesting green space. A new wildlife area is now being developed in the north west. Along the western boundary above the railway line there is a dense growth of mature pedunculate oaks, Lombardy poplars, sycamore and elm trees, but this is closed off to the general public.

Like many parks today Northbrook Park in Lee has a separate, enclosed area for exercising dogs off the lead, and it is a generous and attractive space where dogs and their owners can enjoy themselves.

The mature oak and ash trees in the park and the generous shrub borders create a sense of calm and several new young saplings will ensure the tree cover increases in the future.

Northbrook Park is open, immaculate and interesting and deservedly one of the Green Flag Parks in Lewisham.

Access: Gates on Baring Road
Opening times: 8 am to sunset
Facilities: Children's play area, multipurpose ball court, jogging/walking track, separate dog walking area, trim trail, football pitches, seats
Designation: Green Flag public park, SINC of Local Importance
Size: 3.8 hectares (9.4 acres)
Northbrook Park Community Group: www.facebook.com

Below: Northbrook Park in December

Northbrook Park with outdoor gym gear, children's play area and perimeter paved path

Marching round the circuit with the multipurpose ball court behind

Cheeky chappy watching the people exercising!

Sydenham Cottages Nature Reserve

As the River Quaggy meandered through the countryside it formed a small oxbow lake just off Claypit Lane (today's Marvels Lane). Nearby were cottages which were built in the 1860s for farmworkers employed mainly by Durham Farm, a dairy farm with sixty cows. There were originally eleven cottages, but only six remain today, unusual examples of their type in Lewisham. Outside the first cottage there is an old pump, used to extract water from the river. The lake eventually became silted up and the river was closely confined in a concrete channel.

This little nature reserve is named after the cottages.

Small paths find a way through a dense growth which includes brambles, hawthorn, blackthorn, elder, damson, and coppiced hazel which crowd together under oak and ash trees. Somehow a small grass clearing in the middle of the reserve has escaped the enthusiastically spreading shrubs and trees. The usual birds and insects inhabit the reserve as well as six species of bats, ring-necked parakeets and jays, and of course foxes.

The Green Chain Walk and Capital Ring Walk follow a footpath on the opposite side of the river, separated from the nature reserve by the River Quaggy. The river is not an integral part of the site but there are plans to open it up, similar to the work carried out in Chinbrook Meadows at the instigation of the Quaggy Waterways Action Group.

Until the Quaggy is set free Sydenham Cottages Nature Reserve will continue as a small tangled wildness separated from its brook.

Access: Alice Thompson Close SE12 9PW off Marvels Lane in Grove Park
Opening times: Always open
Facilities: None
Designation: Local Nature Reserve, SINC of Local Importance
Size: 0.72 hectares (1.8 acres)

Dog violets, snowdrops, and lesser celandine at Sydenham Cottages in April

Grassy central area with flowering blackthorn in April

Lee and Lee Green

A thousand years ago the French were the Lords of the Manor in Lee when William the Conqueror gave the manor to his brother Odo, the Bishop of Bayeux. At the time of the *Domesday Book* Lee consisted of 5 acres of meadow and 10 acres of woodland lying along Lee High Road. Lee Green was a neighbouring and smaller parish. The early Anglo-Saxon leah meant a meadow, or a clearing in the woods, and in 1086 the area was farmland watered by the River Quaggy. St Margaret's Church stood at the top of the hill overlooking the river valleys.

The Lord of the Manor sublet land to members of the aristocracy, but as the property of an alien priory the manor was seized by the Crown in the 14th century, and finally passed out of the hands of religious institutions with the dissolution of the monasteries under Henry VIII in the 16th century. Ownership of the Manor of Lee then continued under the Crown, or English aristocracy.

Below: The Cedars today

Historically there were three areas of focus in Lee: Belmont Hill, the Old Road and Lee Green.

In 1878 Robert Butts effused about 'Lee…a most pleasantly situated suburban parish, in the county of Kent, between Lewisham and Blackheath'. And in this countryside, only 6 miles from the centre of London, wealthy bankers and merchants built their country houses in the 17th, 18th and even early 19th centuries. These mansions included Lee Place and the early 17th century Lee Grove, the home of the Brandram family of chemical and paint manufacturers. This was later developed and renamed The Cedars, with beautiful grounds and lakes, and became the home of John Penn, the marine engineer. Pentland House housed the Smith family; The Firs of c.1700 was built for the Papillon family of bankers; the 18th century Dacre House was the home of Sir Samuel Fludyer Bt, a wealthy banker and a Lord Mayor of London, and Belmont of c.1830 was the home of George Ledwell Taylor, a District Surveyor.

F H Hart reports that until the mid-1800s Mr Lucas, a Lord Mayor of London who rented Dacre House and its surrounding farm grew 'early peas …for market; also excellent crops of both red and white wheat, which was sold in market in those times at a high price'. At Manor Farm in the same period there were 'fifty acres of fruit trees of all descriptions, …early Battersea cabbages, … and three acres of water-cress beds next to the Quaggy'.

The change from countryside to dense housing started in 1824 when the Boone Mansion and its lands were sold at auction. The second agent of change was the development of the railways, with the first service running to Lewisham and Blackheath in 1849.

Lee Green was even more undeveloped than Lee.

Leland L Duncan tells us that Lee Road between the two parishes was 'a very rural spot in the early part of the 19th century, with much broom and furze' and led to Lee Green which spread over two acres.

This large open space had a few cottages in its surrounding farmland, but more importantly the original Tiger's Head

Lee Green today, with The Old Tiger's Head pub on the left, the road to Blackheath in the middle, and The New Tiger's Head on the right, now the Blackheath Food Centre

public house was built in the mid-1700s and was the first stagecoach stop out of London. In the early 1800s the pub was known for its bowling green and city gentlemen would play cricket on the green in the summer and then retire to the pub for refreshments. Farmers from the west of London would exchange their goods with their counterparts from the east here, and in 1815 troops marched through Lee Green for three weeks on their way to Waterloo. Bareknuckle fighting was popular here too, and there were annual horse races in Lee Park.

The Quaggy flows through the area and sudden floods were common. Leland L Duncan tells us that at Christmas in 1830 the water was seven feet deep at Lee Green.

Today only Manor House, Pentland House and The Cedars remain and all have a new existence as a library, hostel and flats. Lee was absorbed into Lewisham in 1900 and Lee Green is long-gone, buried under crowded housing and a busy crossroads. Local people are keen on improving the interchange but the flow of traffic makes change difficult. What a pity so much has been lost.

Further reading

Browning, Paul: www.runner500.wordpress.com
Butts, Robert: *Butts' Historical Guide to Lewisham, Ladywell, Lee, Blackheath and Eltham*, 1878, London; republished by the British Library
Duncan, Leland L: *History of the Borough of Lewisham*, 1908, republished FamLoc, 2015
Hart, F H: *History of Lee and its neighbourhood*, 1882, London; republished by Leopold Classic Library

Edith Nesbit Gardens

Posing for the camera!

Edith Nesbit (1858–1924) was a well-known children's author and a poet, and together with her husband, Hubert Bland, she was a co-founder of the Fabian Society. She led an unconventional life and lived in different areas of south east London, amongst other places. For a while the family home was at 8 Dorville Road in Lee which is round the corner from the park named after her. Subsequently the family moved to The Gables on Baring Road and finally settled at Well Hall in Eltham.

In the 19th century the site of the park was Lee Green Farm which was farmed by William Morris. In Lee and Eltham he and Farmer Giles were the big farmers on leasehold land held by the Crown. The fertile pastures were used for dairy farming and the farm was passed down to William Morris' son Richard Morris who seems to have continued until around the 1860s. After this time housing development overtook farming.

This small neighbourhood park dates back to c.1950s and it is easily overlooked. If you find the park you could walk through the gardens on the tarmacked path in less than three minutes. But don't do that.

Instead, wander over the undulating ground and between the many large London planes and sycamore trees, enjoy the shrubberies along the fenced boundaries, and then sit down on one of the benches. Even if you didn't bring any nuts you will soon have the company of greedy and inquisitive squirrels who are always ready to pose for the camera!

And while you are enjoying these small pleasures you will hear children and their parents in the brightly coloured and popular children's play area which is shaded by the trees in the summer.

Access: Leyland Road and Osberton Road SE12 8XA
Opening times: 8 am to sunset
Facilities: Children's playground
Designation: Public Park
Size: 0.5 hectares (1.2 acres)

Chldren's play area in Edith Nesbit Gardens in December

Gilmore Road Triangle

Gilmore Road Triangle in winter

Gilmore Road Triangle is just ten minutes' walk from the shopping centre in Lewisham. But you could live here for a lifetime and never see it.

In 1863 most of the land between today's Lee High Road and Lewisham High Street was College Farm which belonged to Trinity Hospital in Greenwich. The Earl of Northampton founded the Hospital in 1613 and placed it under the administration of the Mercers' Company. From 1868 the Company developed the College Park housing estate on the farmlands.

Henry Corbett started The Lewisham Nursery c.1736 in the same area and it was later taken over by John Russell (1731–94) who built an extremely lucrative business in Lewisham, 'living many years like a gentleman' on his retirement.[12] His sons John and Thomas and son-in-law John Willmott took over from him. The nursery catalogue of 1806 was extensive and showed the nursery even sold exotic plants such as wisteria to Kew Gardens. By 1822 the nursery covered 150 acres, and employed seventy people, but finally closed in 1860.

The OS map of 1870 still shows extensive nursery lands between the railway and Lewisham Park. Could Gilmore Road Triangle further to the north be a little patch of this nursery?

Venture down a tarmacked path off Wisteria Road, between the houses and under huge London plane trees, and you will find yourself on a grassy hillside. A majestic old poplar tree crowns the hilltop and little copses with willows, poplars and lime trees circle the boundaries of the park, intermingled with white hawthorn and flowering pear trees in the spring.

This delightful space is ideal for a few minutes of calm before tackling the vibrant street market nearby where shops sell exotic foods and dressmakers can find the market's must-visit fabric stall!

Access: Wisteria Road SE13 5HN,
Bonfield Road SE13 5EU, and Clarendon Rise SE13 6DL
Opening times: 8 am to sunset
Facilities: None
Designation: SINC of local importance
Size: 0.8 hectares (2 acres)

Gilmore Road Triangle in spring

Manor House Gardens

The Manor House is a Grade II* listed building which was probably built for Thomas Lucas c.1771-72 by Richard Jupp, a notable English architect. Thomas Lucas was a wealthy man with wide-ranging international business interests, the treasurer, then president, of Guy's Hospital and an MP.

In 1798 Sir Francis Baring bought the Manor of Lee, and the Manors of Shroffolds and Bankers, from the Earl of Rockingham. At the Manor House he developed the kitchen gardens of c.3 acres with a fine collection of imported fruit trees. From Sir Francis the manor was passed down through the family, the head of which became the Earl of Northbrook in the mid-1860s.

The family lived mainly in Hampshire and so the Manor House was let. In 1898 Lord Northbrook sold the Manor House and its grounds to the London County Council for a library and public park which opened in 1902. A full and fascinating history of the house is given by the Lee Manor Society and by Paul Browning.[13]

The gardens underwent a major restoration programme in 1999–2000 and are much as originally laid out in 1773. A path from the house curves around the boundaries and skirts the lawns which run down to a large lake. Close to the Manor House is a fascinating 18th century Ice House which opens to the public from 3 pm to 5 pm on the first and third Mondays between May and September in a normal year, and sometimes opens during Open House Weekend in London in the autumn.

Come to this much-loved park if you are feeling lonely. The popular cafe in the grounds offers refreshments and you will find yourself in the company of joggers, friends sitting and chatting, and family groups picnicking on the grass in summer. And there are always children squealing and cavorting in the playground or kicking a ball on the grass.

Lean on the railings at the lakeside and watch the mallards, coots, tufted ducks and even gulls arguing over food. Inevitably there are also Canada geese and the lake is an important feeding source for bats. The swans patrol majestically and keep order and the herons look on disdainfully, as only herons can can!

The front façade of the Manor House

Just beyond the lake the River Quaggy flows between two rows of large willows, sycamores and alders, and beyond the belt of trees are tennis courts, a ball court, and a separate dog exercise area.

The monthly Farmers Market is popular and the park is crowded for the Summer Festival in June. Altogether it is an idyllic country scene viewed from the terraces behind the Manor House.

Access: The Old Road SE13 5TA, Manor Lane, and Brightfield Road
Opening times: 8 am to sunset
Facilities: Pistachios in the Park Cafe and toilets (not open every day), children's playground, tennis courts, multipurpose ball court, outdoor gym gear, separate dog walking area
Designation: Green Flag public park, SINC of Borough Importance
Size: 1.4 hectares (3.5 acres)
Friends of Manor House Gardens: www.facebook.com

The lawns behind the house, leading down to the lake, with the cafe and children's play area on the right

Above: Herons nesting in the lake in January
Below: Male swan clearing the lake around the island to protect his mate who was sitting on a nest

The lake in winter

The cafe and gardens of Manor House Gardens in October

Manor Park

The cafe in Manor Park with a children's play area in the background

In the 1870s there were open fields here which were probably part of Manor Farm. By 1897 the farm was being sold off for residential developments; Manor Park Road was partly laid out and large villas were appearing, but there was still farmland around the farmhouse and Manor House itself. By 1914 the area was completely built up.

The site was a pig farm in the 1950s and 1960s which Lewisham Borough Council then bought together with some land attached to the large houses on Manor Park. In 1966 the park was laid out with shrubberies, rose beds and the usual formal park planting of the time.

Major restoration work was undertaken in 2007 and the River Quaggy now flows into the park at the Longhurst Road entrance alongside a new wetland where the river can spread when the river levels rise. It continues along the side of the park, running quietly over gravel beds and under overhanging willows, poplars and grasses.

Wildflowers such as field scabious and wild carrot are starting to appear, and instead of the formal annual beds of previous times there are two 'sunshine gardens' with drought-tolerant plants such as rosemary, globe thistle, alchemilla, sage, phlomis and thalictrum.

Today this delightful park is one of the hidden green spaces in Lewisham. It is easy to treat this as a shortcut between the shopping centre in Lewisham and residential areas of Lee, but that would be to miss the sound of the river, the swelling buds in spring, and just the sheer charm of this small oasis.

Access: Leahurst Road SE13 5HU, Manor Park SE13 5RL, Weardale Road SE13 5QB, Longhurst Road SE13 5LP
Opening times: 8 am to sunset, depending on the season
Facilities: Children's playground, cafe
Designation: Green Flag public park,
SINC of Borough Importance
Size: c.1.4 hectares (3.5 acres)
Lee Manor Society: www.leemanorsociety.org

The insect weather vanes in Manor Park

Enjoying the park

The River Quaggy in Manor Park at the end of summer

Manor Park in winter

Merchant Taylors' Almshouses

Christopher Boone (1616–1686) was a wealthy wool merchant and a member of the Worshipful Company of Merchant Taylors who in 1670 settled in Lee Place, a partially moated red brick building on the Old Road. In 1680 he bought land to build to build almshouses. He may have commissioned Sir Christopher Wren to design the buildings but it is thought the work was actually done by his colleague Robert Hooke who was also a Merchant Taylor. Four houses were built in 1683, one for a school teacher, the others for poor elderly people, as well as a chapel which was intended as a mausoleum for Boone and his wife; the Boone family vault in St Margaret's Churchyard was built later.

The Worshipful Company of Merchant Taylors were the Trustees of the Boone Almshouses which were funded by further donations from Christopher Boone — rental income from land near Dacres House and from a farm in Hereford. The almshouses were demolished in 1876 and replaced by new almshouses (demolished in 2014) further towards Lee Green, but the original chapel remains, a Grade 1 listed building which was renovated in 2008.

Lee Place was demolished when the estate was sold in 1824. This was a real tragedy: 'the interior of the principal rooms was wainscoted with oak and Spanish chestnut beautifully carved and polished;….various implements used in the farm and garden, beautifully carved by Grinling Gibbons…hung there in festoons'.[14]

In 1826 the Merchant Taylors bought land from the Boone estate and built an additional thirty almshouses behind the original homes on Lee Road. 'The land and plantations were tastefully laid out by Messrs Willmot, of the old Lewisham Nursery, and have always been beautifully kept by the resident gardener….the present gardener [1882] has improved the flower beds very much by bedding out geraniums and planting a variety of beautiful annuals in front of the shrubbery'.[15]

The residents had a fruit garden where they grew elderberries for wine, and pears and apples, with water from a stream fed by a spring on the top of the hill.

The site was sold by the Merchant Taylors in c.2010 to fund new almshouses nearby and the buildings and grounds are currently being redeveloped by a private developer. It is to be hoped the new gardens will be as fruitful as those of the past on this historically important site.

Access: Brandram Road SE13 5RT, but there is no access to this site at present

Below: The Merchant Taylors' coat of arms on the gatepost next to the chapel

Above: The original Boone's Chapel on Lee High Road
Below: The garden behind Boone's Chapel

Above: Gateway into the almshouses from Brandram Road
Below: Part of the almshouses, now a building site

St Margaret's Old Churchyard

The first church on this site was dedicated to St Margaret of Antioch, and built in c.1080 with the valleys of the River Quaggy to the south and the Upper Kid Brook to the north. Today only the west tower remains and it is a Grade II listed building. According to F H Hart the first church was a small chalk and flint building which seated 150 people. A rectory was built to the west of the church in 1636.

The original church was finally demolished in 1813 and a second, bigger church for 500 people was built by Joseph Gwilt on the same foundations but it collapsed.

The third, even bigger church was built in 1839–41 by John Brown of Norwich on the opposite side of the road. The old rectory and 0.75 acres of land around the original church were sold to John Penn of The Cedars in 1866. The new church was enlarged in 1876 and this is the Grade II* listed building which we find today.

It is fascinating to wander amongst the graves and imagine the people who once lived here. The Astronomers Royal Edmond Halley, Nathaniel Bliss and John Pond were buried in the old churchyard. Other tombs include members of the Boone family of Lee Place, Lord Dacre of Dacre Place, and Thomas Lucas and Sir John Call of the Manor House. And then there is Cocking who fell out of Charles Green's balloon, in a parachute, and killed himself in a field off Burnt Ash Hill on 24 July 1837.

Like many old graveyards St Margaret's churchyard is peaceful, softened by the trees and with a strong sense of the layers of time.

Access: Lee Terrace SE13 5DL
Opening times: Old churchyard temporarily closed to the public; new churchyard always open
Facilities: None
St Margaret's, Lee: www.stmargaretslee.org.uk

Above: The Boone family tomb with the new church in the background

The remains of the old church tower, looking down the former nave, with a hint of The Cedars in the background

CENTRAL LEWISHAM

In the central section we find the town centre of Lewisham, Ladywell, Brockley and Crofton Park, Catford, Rushey Green and Hither Green. Historically Catford and Rushey Green were part of central Lewisham but Mountsfield Park (no.60) is included in South and South East Lewisham because of the Forster family connection, and Hither Green nature reserve (no.59) because of the connection to the 20th century development of most of Catford and Hither Green.

John Coulter suggests Lewisham may have been founded as early as the 7th century by a Jute called Leof or Lefse, or other variations of the name which means the farmstead or home of Leof or Lefse.

In Saxon times the Manor of Lewisham included Greenwich and Woolwich and in 964 the manor was given to the Benedictine Abbey of St Peter in Ghent by King Edgar as a reward for sheltering Dunstan, the Archbishop of Canterbury. A priory was built in Lewisham and its location was thought to be in Rushey Green. The Abbots in Belgium were Lords of the Manor for the next 450 years but it was an unsettled relationship. The Abbey appears to have had a loose control over the land which was divided and sold into the smaller manors of Bankers, Shroffold, Brockley, Catford, Bellingham and possibly Sydenham. By 1066 the Manor no longer included Woolwich. As an alien priory it was more than once seized by the Crown until in 1414 Henry V gave the Manor of Lewisham to the Carthusian Priory of Shene. Finally the church's control of religious institutions and their lands ended with the dissolution of the monasteries by Henry VIII in 1536–40.

From the 14th to the 17th centuries the inhabitants of Lewisham were mainly small farmers and so the large common fields were very important for grazing cattle and the collection of firewood. The common fields were:
- Sundermead (Cornmill Gardens and around Lewisham station)
- Northfield covered 40 acres of a field called Strodes which today is the Brockley and Ladywell Cemeteries. These two fields were probably in the Manor of Bankers.
- Southfield was 42 acres (Lewisham Park and the Lewisham Memorial Garden)
- Clangors covered 32 acres at Rushey Green and would have been in the Manor of Catford
- Broadfield was 80 acres between today's Catford Bridge and Lower Sydenham, and even in 1908 was still farmland
- Westfield is more difficult to identify but may have been a 42 acre field called Pickthornes in Forest Hill.

In 1624 James I gave all his rights to his favourite, The Earl of Holderness, the first of a succession of absentee landlords. In 1673 Admiral George Legge, later Baron Dartmouth, bought the Manor of Lewisham and the family has retained control of the manor since then.

But times were changing. Industries were developing around the mills, the mix of the population was moving towards more manufacturers and professional people, and farming was declining. A few roads were built and improved in the late 18th century.

'Lewisham [in the early 1800s] consisted of the villas round Blackheath, a few shops and cottages in the High Street, interspersed with larger houses standing in their own grounds, and small hamlets at Perry Hill, Sydenham and Southend. There were practically no side roads to the High Street, which was unpaved, and the stream with the elm trees on its banks down the western side gave it a rural appearance not without points of beauty.'[16]

The big changes came in the 19th century. The Enclosure Act of 1819 allowed all remaining common and waste ground in Lewisham to be enclosed and the land was divided between existing landowners: Trinity College, Lord Dartmouth, Lord Eliot, Elise Desvignes, William Prest, the Collyers and Sir Francis Baring. (Between 1761 and 1844 there were c.2,000 Acts of Parliament which supported enclosure of common land.) London's increasing population needed to be housed, new railway stations opened in Lewisham and Blackheath in 1849 and by the turn of the 20th century nearly all the large mansions in Lewisham and Rushey Green had been demolished for new housing, the demographic of the population was different, land ownership had changed and the area had become an urban settlement rather than countryside.

Further reading:

Coulter, John: *Lewisham, History and Guide*, 1994, Alan Sutton Publishing Limited
Duncan, Leland L: *A History of Lewisham*, 1882
Browning, Paul: www.runner500.wordpress.com

The Old Vicarage in Lewisham, rebuilt by the Vicar, George Stanhope, in 1692–93

Lewisham Park

Lewisham Park and the streets immediately surrounding it were once the 42 acres of Southfield in the Manor of Lewisham. This was Lammas Land which means it was grown for half the year, cropped for hay, and then opened for common grazing on 1 August, Lammas Day. The field was part of the Dartmouth Estate and the Marsh Improvement Act of 1844 allowed for Lammas Land to be enclosed and built over.

In 1849 the first railway station opened in Lewisham and Blackheath, enabling affluent professional people to live in the countryside and speedily travel to work in the centre of London. Viscount Lewisham (Lord Dartmouth and the Lord of the Manor) developed Lewisham Park to attract these affluent buyers, and of course to make money. Building work started in the 1840s and the villa at no.78 Lewisham Park, which still stands today, was one of the first houses on the site. Nearby is a mature Scots pine tree which also dates from the original planting at that time.

The development was completed by 1906 and consisted of large detached or semi-detached homes around a central park. The park was for the exclusive use of the residents and was planted with ornamental trees such as weeping ash, tulip trees, horse chestnuts, variegated hollies and shrubs. Limes, chestnuts and London plane trees lined the streets and today are towering and mature.

Lord Dartmouth made a Deed of Arrangement in 1878 for six residents to act as Trustees and be responsible for the maintenance of the park but by the mid-20th century the Trustees apparently couldn't afford the maintenance any longer. In 1959 Lewisham Council bought the freehold of the land and in 1965 the Trustees gave it to the Council for a public park.

The Council retained the trees and added lawns and flower beds, and a formal, terraced garden in the central sunken area (formerly a gravel pit) where they planted roses. They built a children's playground, a refreshment kiosk and toilets, and a flat for a groundsman. The railings around the park, topped with metal hoops, date from the same time.

Today the formal rose garden in the sunken area has been replaced with grass and it is encircled on three sides by beautiful London plane trees; the trees on the fourth side were brought down by the hurricane of 1987.

A meadow alongside the tower blocks supports wildflowers and butterflies and the park has a large bird population. The avenue of cherry trees is replanted and gorgeous in the spring, and there are still some roses and beds of hardy perennials instead of annual bedding plants. The children have a playground but their paddling pool has been replaced with a ball court. The groundsman has gone and the park is maintained by Glendale.

This is a beautiful and elegant park which feels wonderfully spacious. The local people are very lucky indeed.

Access: Several gates around the park give access from Lewisham Park Road
Opening times: 8 am to sunset
Facilities: Children's playground, seats
Designation: Public park
Size: 4.13 hectares (10 acres)

Opposite: The semi-circle of London plane trees in late autumn
Overleaf: The park in spring

Lewisham Memorial Gardens

On 19th century maps this area is a strip of vegetation between the main road (Lewisham High Street) and the front gardens of villas on the Lewisham Park development. After WWI the Earl of Dartmouth and the Trustees donated the land to Lewisham Borough Council and the War Memorial was unveiled in May 1921 by Major General Sir William Thwaites. Edward Albert Stone, a London architect, designed the memorial which is Grade II listed.

The Memorial Gardens were finally laid out in 1963. The gardens are grassed, with crazy paving paths, and are always very neat and tidy. The symmetry of the design and the traditional bedding seem appropriate here with seasonal planting always giving a splash of colour. Yew is cut into low columns, creating small alcoves in which there are seats. At the south end of the gardens the Mayor of Lewisham planted an Indian cedar tree in March 1985 to celebrate the 40th anniversary of the ending of WWII and the founding of the United Nations, and mature London plane trees line the pavement along the road.

What is unusual about these gardens is the memorial to recipients of the Victoria Cross who were associated with Lewisham. Queen Victoria created the Victoria Cross in 1856 to recognise 'valour in the presence of the enemy'. It is the highest and most prestigious award for members of the British Armed Services and only 1,358 VCs have ever been awarded; six are commemorated here.

Brigadier General Clifford Coffin was a heavily decorated and distinguished soldier in WWI, the first general officer to be awarded the VC. After the war he had a distinguished military career. Francis Harvey RM VC died at sea on HMS Lion in 1916; Lt Alan Jerrard was in the RFC and awarded the VC for actions in Italy in 1918; Lt Richard Jones VC died on Vimy Ridge in 1916, aged nineteen years, and he has no known grave; Private John Lynn VC died of gas poisoning at Ypres in 1915, aged twenty-seven years, and he is buried in Belgium; Captain Walter Stone VC was only aged twenty-six when he died at Cambrai and he has no known grave.

Reading about the bravery of these men is sobering and it is worth lingering at the memorial for a few minutes to reflect on their actions and the situations in which they found themselves. In Laurence Binyon's words:

At the going down of the sun and in the morning
We will remember them

Access: Lewisham High Street SE13 7LQ
Opening times: Always open
Facilities: seats
Designation: Public park
Size: 0.5 hectares (1.2 acres)

Below: The Victoria Cross Memorial in Lewisham Memorial Gardens

Lewisham Memorial Gardens in April

St Mary's Churchyard

There has been a church on this site since the late 11th century when the first church was probably built by the Abbey of St Peter in Ghent, in Belgium. However, the oldest remaining part of today's church is the base of the tower which dates from 1498–1512. The current Church of St Mary the Virgin was designed by George Gibson Junior and built in 1774–77, with the interior remodelled by A W Blomfield in 1881–82 and it is a Grade II* listed building.

The Church of St Mary the Virgin was the parish church for the Manor of Lewisham and the graveyard was extended several times before it was finally closed. Several notable people were buried here including Henry Tibbats Stainton (d.1892), who was a significant entomologist and expert on butterflies and moths, and who lived in Mountsfield House; Ephraim How, the cutler at Southend Pond; Ebenezer Blackwell (d.1782), a banker and a partner in Martin's Bank, lived at The Limes which was on the site of today's Roman Catholic Church in Lewisham High Street. He and his wife were friends of John Wesley who was a frequent visitor to their home. Captain Charles Weller (d.1866) was a captain with the East India Company's merchant fleet, an owner of one of the trading ships, the *Albion*, and an Elder Brother of Trinity House.

The churchyard was laid out as a public garden in 1886. Today the old churchyard is known for the many fern species around the tombstones and in the walls, including the male fern, harts-tongue fern, black spleenwort, wall rue, maidenhair spleenwort and the holly fern. Quite a collection!

An avenue of yew trees leads from Lewisham High Street to the back of the church. There are also hornbeams, sycamores, cherries, oak, holly and silver birch, and even an Indian bean tree in the churchyard.

The Therapeutic Garden lies behind the church and alongside the River Ravensbourne. This was a burial ground until 1856 after which it gradually deteriorated. In 2014 volunteers from the church started clearing the ground and the Therapeutic Garden opened in 2017.

The gardens are now managed by church volunteers and patients from the Ladywell Unit which is part of the South London and Maudsley NHS Trust (SLaM) and which uses gardening to promote mental wellbeing.

The old churchyard is fascinating. As you walk through the gate the layers of time envelop you and in the new Therapeutic Garden, away from the sound of the traffic, there is a real sense of healing.

Access: Lewisham High Street SE13 6LE
Opening times: 8 am to sunset
Facilities: Seats
Designation: Churchyard and community garden, SINC of Borough Importance
Size: 0.89 hectares (2.2 acres)
St Mary's Church: www.lewishamparish.com

The Therapeutic Garden in early April

The Portico of St Mary

The tomb of Captain Weller

Left: Harts-tongue fern and black spleenwort in the church wall

Middle: Squirrels abound!

Bottom: Bird bath in the gardens

The Therapeutic Garden behind the Church of St Mary in June

Slagrove Place

In the 19th century Ladywell Village was a few cottages at the bottom of Vicar's Hill alongside the bridge over the River Ravensbourne. The wooden bridge was for foot traffic; horses and carts crossed via a ford until 1830 when the wooden bridge was replaced with brick. The bridge was widened further in 1857 to accommodate the railway line.

At the same time the well here, which had been used since the 15th century, disappeared under the arches of the bridge. The well was possibly named after the Virgin Mary as the Church of St Mary is close by. There was a second spring further west which disappeared when sewers were installed in the area; the site is marked by a plaque at no.148 Ladywell Road and the water was reputedly of benefit to those with weak eyes.

The area to the north of Ladywell, around Vicar's Hill, was the vicar's glebe land and pastures until c.1882 when Algernon Road was laid down. On the south side of Ladywell Road, just beyond the village, was Slagrave Farm (yes, a different spelling!), and beyond that, further west, was Bridge House Farm which was on land owned by the Bridge House Trust and which overlapped into Brockley.

In the 18th century the poor and needy turned to the church for support and parishes established workhouses which offered basic accommodation (indoor relief) or help with clothing or some food or heating (outdoor relief). But help was inconsistent, even brutal, and the Poor Law of 1834 aimed to introduce parity of care. Parishes were required to group together in Unions managed by a Board of Guardians and build workshouses.

St Olave's Union was set up in March 1836 and managed an existing workhouse on Parish Street in Bermondsey. In 1868 the Board of Guardians took on responsibility for more workhouses in Rotherhithe which provided hospital care for the elderly poor who were sick. This included building new hospitals.

In 1894 Slagrave Farm, of c.35 acres, was sold to the St Olave's Union Board of Guardians and in 1897–1900 the Union built the Ladywell Institution. In today's terms this would be a residential home for the elderly, with accommodation and medical care facilities, the first

Above: The remaining central block of the former Bermondsey Institution
Below: The gates of the former Institution

institution of its kind. The Ladywell Workhouse (later known as the Bermondsey Institution) had 812 beds, and the site included a water tower, laundry, hospital and two chapels.

In 1904 the Union was renamed the Parish of Bermondsey and the buildings in Ladywell were used as the Bermondsey Military Hospital in WWI. In 1930 the institution was taken over by the London County Council and continued as a Residential Home until 1975.

Today most of the buildings have been demolished apart from part of the administration block, the water tower, the stables, the gatehouse and the impressive entrance gates to the institution. Slagrove Place Estate is a housing estate from 1995 built on the institution grounds and overlooking a large green which was once the institution's recreation area. The green was saved through a strong campaign supported by local people and led by the Ladywell Society.

Support and care for the homeless continues at Slagrove Place through Sanctuary Supported Living and at Lloyd Court Almshouses.

Access: Slagrove Place SE13 7HS
Opening times: Always open
Facilities: None
Designation: Public open space

Below: The green at Slagrove Place

Brockley and Crofton Park

Brocele was an early name for the area and Broc is the Anglo-Saxon for a badger so maybe the name referred to an area where badgers could be found? Or perhaps it was named after Broca who had a clearing in the woods? Historically Brockley stretched from Deptford in the north down to Forest Hill in the south, and just south of Lewisham Way and Stanstead Road (the South Circular Road) are useful boundaries for the book.

Upper Brockley in the north was rural and the land was poor pastureland. But as London started to expand in the early 1700s there was an increased demand for food and market gardening became more lucrative, especially when the land could be enriched with night soil from London. Gardeners in Brockley were particularly known for their strawberries, rhubarb and pears.

The opening of the London and Croydon railway in 1839, replacing the Croydon Canal, marked the beginning of change. While market gardening continued during the 19th century land in upper Brockley was disappearing under two large housing estates on land belonging to the Wickham family and the Tyrwhitt-Drake family. The Bridge House Trust was also a private landowner and the large landowners in the southern part of the area were Christ's Hospital and the Earl of St Germans. All would eventually develop housing or sell land in the area.

Crofton Park is the site of the original hamlet of Brockley in the 18th century and the main buildings in the hamlet were Brockley Hall, the Brockley Jack (rebuilt in 1898) and Brockley Farm.

Left: The Brockley Barge pub

When a new railway station opened in 1892 there was already a station at Brockley and so a different name was needed. There doesn't seem to be an historical reason for choosing Crofton Park but this distinguished the station from Brockley Station and the area was renamed accordingly, possibly by a local property developer.

There have been several Brockley Farms over the centuries, one of which was the 16th century Forest Place which was demolished in the 1870s. The name reminds us that this area was once part of the Great North Wood. An old road ran from the docks in Deptford, up Deptford High Street (previously Butt Lane), Tanners Hill, Upper Brockley Road to Brockley Cross and then to the Brockley Jack on Brockley Green. From here the lane continued to Forest Hill. The lane was used to take timber from the Great North Wood to the dockyards in Deptford when Henry VIII started developing his navy.

The origins of Brockley Hall are not known, but estate agent details for Brockley House in the early 1800s describe a large and handsome country house set in extensive grounds of c.13 acres. In the 1840s John Thompsett Noakes bought the property and renovated the house which was subsequently known as Brockley Hall. He was a brewer who owned the Brockley Jack pub, opposite Brockley Hall. Maude Noakes was the last member of the family and when she died in 1931 the mansion was demolished and its grounds were developed as housing. The extensive Noakes business was bought by Courage in the 1930s.

In the 18th century the Brockley Jack was known as The Crooked Billet; in the early 19th century it was The Castle and reputedly a haunt of highwaymen. The name changed to The Brockley Jack in the mid-1800s and the pub was rebuilt in 1898, an unpopular move, because the old building looked very atmospheric in paintings and drawings. Today the building also houses the Brockley Jack Theatre.

Further reading:

Spurgeon, Darrell: *A History of Brockley in 10½ blogs*; www.brockleycentral.blogspot.com
Crofton Park History: www.croftonparkhistory.com

Above: The Noakes family tomb in Ladywell Cemetery
Below: The Brockley Jack pub

Blythe Hill Fields

Above and opposite: Very early morning on Blythe Hill Fields in April

Wow! What a wonderful view!

Blythe Hill Fields crowns a hill which is 70 metres high and offers views of Canary Wharf on the Isle of Dogs, the Shard in central London, Shooters Hill and even the North Downs on a clear day. And the landscape of leafy suburbs between Brockley and the River Thames is perhaps surprising to those who regard London as streets of dull houses and tall office blocks.

A Roman road passed this way 2,000 years ago and when you stand at the crossroads on top of the hill you can almost hear the tramp of feet. The London to Lewes Way was 71kms in length from Watling Street in Peckham to Lewes and dates from the 1st to the 2nd century. The diagonal path which enters from Codrington Road, over the top of Blythe Hill Fields and down Blythe Hill Lane, is on the route of the road.

In the 19th century much of the hill was on Brockley Farm which lay to the north. Blythe Hill House was built to the south in 1842 between Montem Road and Blythe Hill Lane, and its grounds also extended over part of Blythe Hill. The house was demolished in 1895.

Job Heath's brickworks office was in Holdenby Road and the clay was dug in a pit on the north of the hill where Stillness Road, Codrington Hill and Crofton Park Road come together today. The chimney of the brick kilns was only demolished in 1938.

The London County Council bought the land and opened a public park in 1935. Today this large park has grasslands rich in wildflowers and semi-mature acers and hornbeams

The Friends of Blythe Hill Fields actively fundraise and promote events in the park. This is a delightful hill for an evening stroll in the setting sun or a very early morning walk before the rush of the day.

Access: Blythe Hill Lane SE23 1SP, Montacute Road, Codrington Hill, Brockley View
Opening times: Always open
Facilities: Trim Trail, Children's play area, table tennis table, seats
Designation: Public open space
Size: 7 hectares (17.3 acres)
Friends of Blythe Hill Fields: www.blythehillfields.org.uk

Breakspears Mews Community Garden

In addition to the four main monastic orders there were several semi-monastic orders which based themselves on the writings of St Augustine and are generally known as Canons Regular. These were priests who lived in monasteries but worked in the community. A very important group of Canons Regular were the Premonstratensians who were founded by St Norbert of the Abbey of Prémontré and they arrived in England in 1130.

In 1182 a Premonstratensian Abbey was founded in Brockley, probably on the site surrounding today's Beverley Court and St Peter's Church. The Canons Regular were given the Manor of Brockley which they retained when they moved to Bayham Abbey in Sussex in 1205. The Abbey and its possessions were seized by the Crown in 1526, shortly before the main dissolution of the monasteries.

There are two interesting associations here: the Abbey was an Augustinian order and the only English Pope, Nicholas Breakspear, was an Augustinian; and one of the Drake family, who were major landowners in Brockley, married Miss Ashby whose family home was Breakspear House in Harefield.

In the 18th century Manor Farm covered c.80 acres and was accessed off Wickham Road in Brockley. The farm house stood just north of today's St Peter's Court surrounded by fields and orchards. Joseph Myatt took on the farm as a tenant farmer in 1827 having previously specialised in growing rhubarb in Camberwell. Rhubarb had been regarded as medicinal in earlier centuries but Myatt grew rhubarb for eating and produced two high-yielding varieties, Victoria (1837) and Linnaeus (c.1842) which he sold at Covent Garden and elsewhere. Myatt experimented with strawberries too and in 1831 introduced the prize-winning pine-apple strawberry which was followed by other new varieties. The annual strawberry feasts at the farm were one of the year's social events in the area! But London was expanding and in 1853 the farmland was sold for housing. Joseph Myatt died in 1855 and was buried in Nunhead Cemetery.

By the 21st century the southern side of Breakspears Mews had become a disgusting rubbish dump and a small group of local residents and the Brockley Society decided to transform the site. They approached the Council and eventually gained planning permission for change of use to a Community Garden in May 2012. The team negotiated a lease with Lewisham Council and secured funds from the Mayor's Fund. The rubbish was cleared on 8th March 2013, raised beds were installed, and vegetable and fruit growing started.

It is good to see the continuation of purpose for the site and surely Joseph Myatt would have approved?

Access: Ashby Road SE4 1PX or St Peter's Court, Wickham Road SE4 1NE
Opening times: Check the website
Facilities: None
Designation: Community garden
Friends of Breakspears Mews Community Garden:
w.brockleysociety.org.uk/breakspears-mews-community-garden/

Pumpkin growing well in one of the raised beds

Sally and Elaine discussing the vegetables one Thursday evening in July

Brockley Cemetery and Ladywell Cemetery

A cemetery as a garden? This seems unlikely but today many of these old burial grounds have become wild gardens or even nature reserves. Of course they are also sacred places, truly gardens of remembrance.

Brockley Cemetery was originally Deptford New Cemetery and the new graveyard for St Paul's Church in Deptford when the graveyard there closed in 1858. Both Brockley Cemetery and Ladywell Cemetery were laid out by Tinkler & Morphew, who were architects and surveyors, and opened in 1858. At the time they were separated by a plant nursery and a wall; today both have gone and a grassy ridge has replaced the wall.

As you walk through the gates on Brockley Road a feeling of calm envelops you. The area on Ivy Lane (an old footpath and now a road) and along the old boundary between the two cemeteries is particularly enchanting.

The cemetery is filled with beautiful old London plane trees, horse chestnuts, beeches and poplars, many of which were planted when the cemetery was first landscaped.

If you look carefully you can find cow parsley, garlic mustard and green alkanet in the shade. Cuckooflower, sedges, oxeye daisies, vetches, birds-foot-trefoil, buttercups and several other wildflowers have been identified and the cemetery walls are home to holly fern, harts-tongue fern, black spleenwort and stonecrops and lichens. The Friends post a full list of plants on their website.

The old graves are surrounded by this garden and close to the houses on Merritt Road a new, small woodland burial site is hidden away.

There are 195 war graves in Brockley Cemetery, mostly in a separate war plot, and a memorial wall lists those who do not have headstones. The memorial to civilians who died in the wars reminds us of the dreadful bombing of London during the Blitz. A separate Roman Catholic cemetery stands on one side, but both the Anglican memorial chapel and the Roman Catholic chapel by Pugin were destroyed in WWII in the same air raid.

Above and opposite: Brockley Cemetery in late April

Above: The Kipling stone for Lieutenant James Ernest Kirkham Bell of the 8th Battalion Border Regiment, died 5 August 1916, aged twenty years, stands in front of the family grave. Alongside is the grave of Corporal Cyril Potts, who died on the first day of the Battle of the Somme, aged twenty-eight, and his family.

Above: The tomb of Jane Maria Clouson who was murdered in 1871. Edmund Pook was charged but found not guilty.

Ladywell Cemetery was originally Lewisham Cemetery but was renamed in 1914. The chapel of 1858 is nonconformist and was built by an unknown architect; the Anglican chapel was destroyed by bombing in WWII.

There are fewer trees in Ladywell Cemetery and in some areas the graves are in rigidly straight lines, but in the older sections of the cemetery the trees and meandering paths convey a more peaceful and gentle atmosphere.

There are 226 war graves from WWI and eighteen from WWII in Ladywell Cemetery. A war graves plot lists 100 names on its memorial wall, and the Commonwealth War Graves Commission cares for a small plot along the south wall of the cemetery with a further 46 headstones to those killed during the World Wars.

While Ladywell Cemetery is perhaps more austere than its neighbours both the sites are very beautiful and bring to mind the words of Ernest Dowson who is buried here:

> *They are not long, the days of wine and roses:*
> *Out of a misty dream*
> *Our path emerges for a while, then closes*
> *Within a dream.*

Access: From Brockley Road SE4 2QY
and Ladywell Road SE13 7HY
Opening times: 10 am to 4 pm or 5 pm depending on the season
Facilities: Toilets and a Chapel in Ladywell Cemetery
Designation: SINC of Borough Importance Grade 1
Size: 14.87 hectares (37 acres)
Brockley and Ladywell Cemeteries:
www.lewisham.gov.uk/organizations/brockley-cemetery

In a corner of Brockley Cemetery

The chapel in Ladywell Cemetery with the memorial plot to those killed in the World Wars, a memorial wall to civilians killed in the wars, and the grave of Driver Arthur Atkins of Lewisham (d.11.3.1917) in the foreground

Brockley Station Community Garden

A small but stunning garden has been created on the side of the railway embankment leading up to Brockley Station. The garden and station are on Coulgate Street which is pedestrianised and offers several cafes with outdoor seating. The Brockley Barge pub is just round the corner.

The Brockley Station Community Garden is an initiative of the Brockley Cross Action Group working with Lewisham Council, the railway authorities and local Councillors. It is now maintained by the Brockley Cross Action Group.

The garden is on derelict railway land and it was designed as a haven for both people and wildlife. The cheerful space has new steps, a ramp up to the station, a clever planting of shrubs, perennials and grasses, a wildlife area, an edible garden and a new woodland area planted in 2020. The vegetation is purposely kept low to ensure good visibility and safety.

This charming little garden shows very clearly what local people can do for themselves to enrich their lives and the lives of those who live in their community and it is a remarkable lesson to others living in Lewisham.

Access: Brockley Railway Station and Coulgate Street
Opening times: Always open
Facilities: Cafes on Coulgate Street
Designation: Public open space
Brockley Cross Action Group: www.brockleycrossactiongroup.co.uk

Below: Perennials, grasses, and wildflowers on the embankment
Opposite: Looking down Coulgate Street with cafes on the left and at the far end

Crofton Park Railway Garden

This little garden is another heart-warming story about a community determined to rescue unused land and improve the surroundings of local residents.

In 2012 the railway company of the time agreed that local residents could tackle a piece of derelict dumping ground next to Crofton Park Station and develop a garden. The residents established a Community Organisation and raised the necessary money, Mark Lane helped design the garden and Verde Landscapes undertook the work to create a community space. To fund ongoing costs the Friends organise a monthly Community Market at the site.

It is worth a train journey to Crofton Park Railway Station to see how an ugly and unloved space has been transformed into an attractive and productive garden which is enjoyed by local people.

Access: Marnock Road SE4 1EU
Opening times: Monday to Saturday, 9 am to 5 pm
Closed Bank Holidays and Sundays
Facilities: Cafes on Brockley Road
Designation: Undesignated public open space
Friends of Crofton Park Railway Garden:
www.croftonparkrailwaygarden.org.uk

Below and opposite: Crofton Park Railway Garden in summer

Frendsbury Gardens

The London Chatham and Dover Railway ran to the east of Ivydale Road in 1898 and divided roughly where Pincott Place begins today. The line heading south was the High Level railway from Nunhead to Crystal Palace which was lifted in 1956 but the line heading east towards Crofton Park Railway Station remains in use. Frendsbury Garden is situated between the two railway lines.

As the years passed the site became a fly-tipping rubbish dump until local residents and Lewisham Council came together and decided to make a community garden. Money was raised from the Big Lottery Fund, Lewisham Council and other sources and the new garden, known as Pincott Place People's Park, opened in 2009. In 2013 the garden was awarded a Green Flag. It is not clear when the name changed.

Today Frendsbury Gardens (as it is now known) is used by hundreds of local people as a space to relax, a place to learn and play or even just as a shortcut on a journey. The garden is maintained mainly by the Friends who are all local residents and everyone in the neighbourhood is encouraged to have a voice in how the garden is managed and its programme of activities and events.

Frendsbury Gardens belongs to the Capital Growth Campaign and offers healthy eating courses which teach people how to cook the food they grow, and gardening sessions to people with mental health difficulties, taking referrals from local health services and Sydenham Garden.

This pretty and developing garden is the result of community determination and an example to residents in other unloved corners of Lewisham.

Access: Frendsbury Road E4 2BL
Opening times: 8 am to sunset
Facilities: Clubhouse, shelter, seats, outdoor kitchen
Designation: Community Garden
Friends of Frendsbury Gardens: www.frendsbury.wordpress.com

Above: Art installations in the gardens

Perennial sunflowers

Grapes

Nasturtiums

Uchi Kuri squash

Above: The shelter and meeting room
Below: The workshop with a local mural

Hilly Fields

By the end of the 19th century inner-city areas were crowded and unhealthy, and Charles Booth had identified the worst area in London as Greenwich, which included Deptford.

Octavia Hill, one of the founders of the National Trust, was working to improve the conditions of people in poor areas and she was active in Deptford. When she heard of plans to build at Hilly Fields (or Vicar's Hill as it had been known since at least the 16th century) she rallied the support of the Commons Preservation Society, the Kyrle Society and the Metropolitan Public Gardens Association and she and her Committee persuaded the London County Council to buy the land for a public park.

The park, which opened in 1896, was designed by Lt Col J J Sexby who describes paths, a bandstand, a cricket pitch and lots of open space for general recreation and for children to play. The Francis Drake Bowls Club opened in 1906.

An old footpath from Lewisham Way (alongside K J Building Supplies) led behind the houses on Tyrwhitt Road into Whitepost Lane, lined up with the path past the Bowls Club and continued over the hill and down Vicars Hill Road to Ladywell. The area immediately below the lane was a limekiln and brickfields and a pottery stretched down to the railway at the end of Brookbank Road from the late 18th century to late 19th century. Even in 1882 today's cricket pitch in Hilly Fields was a brickfield! John and Henry Lee owned the land and worked the brickfields and John Lee lived in Ellerslie House, now the site of Grover Court on Lewisham Way.

The West Kent Grammar School was built on top of the hill in 1884–85 and it was taken over by Prendergast School in 1995 when the school moved from its original site in Catford. New school buildings have since been added on Adelaide Avenue. The Worshipful Company of Leathersellers funded the original site for Prendergast School and its move to Hilly Fields, and the school is part of the Leathersellers' Federation of Schools.

Mature London plane trees line Hilly Fields Crescent in the north and at the top of Eastern Road. In the south east of the park an area of natural woodland with ash, oak, hawthorn and blackthorn hides near the Hilly Fields Stone Circle which was created to mark the Millennium, and which is also a sundial. Its twelve granite boulders are over 400 million years old and the two tall standing stones are called St Norbert's Gate. St Norbert was the founder of the Premonstratensian order of Canons Regular, the order which established an Abbey in Brockley in the 12th century. (See no.42 Breakspears Mews Community Garden.)

The Friends of Hilly Fields are improving the meadow along Adelaide Avenue and have planted and are caring for new trees on the eastern side of the park in The Copse. The little orchard below the Stone Circle was planted in 2012 and they are introducing the traditional craft of hedge laying in the boundary hedges.

Below: Exercising in the park against a backdrop of Canary Wharf

Looking towards The Shard at London Bridge on an early May evening

Above: The woodland area of Hilly Fields
Below: The Stone Circle at Hilly Fields with Prendergast School behind

Above: Black-billed magpie in the Hilly Fields Woods
Opposite: Friends, and the view from Hilly Fields towards Blythe Hill Fields and One Tree Hill

This is a wide and open park with lovely views but it also has hidden corners which are fun to explore. And when you are finished exploring, exercising or walking the cafe offers a seat and delicious refreshments.

Access: The park is unfenced and can be accessed from Adelaide Avenue, Montague Avenue, Vicars Hill and Hilly Fields Crescent
Opening times: Always open
Facilities: Three tennis courts, a cricket pitch, a basketball court, a football pitch, and a popular cafe, seats and picnic tables.
Designation: Green Flag public park, SINC of Local Importance
Size: 18.2 hectares (45 acres)
Friends of Hilly Fields: www.hilly.org.uk

Ravensbourne Park Gardens

Ravensbourne Park Gardens is a small green space which is about a five-minute walk from the river. Its origin is linked to the development of the Ravensbourne Park Estate which started in the 1820s and was intended to provide luxury housing with the park as a private green for the local residents — perhaps the developers were copying the select London squares? This was an area of substantial mansions in large grounds with homes such as Ravensbourne Park House, Blythe House, Hillfields House and Summerfield House.

The Mid-Kent railway line was built in the mid-1800s and the station at Catford Bridge opened in 1857. Despite the opening of the railway new houses only appeared slowly, picking up as the cost of train travel into London decreased towards the end of the century.

A few of the original homes still stand on Ravensbourne Park (the road), including the villas at 60–62 whose gardens are now Iona Close Orchard.

The park is quiet and neat and particularly pretty in early summer. It is grassed, with some fine, mature London plane trees as well as a few ornamental trees.

Access: Ravensbourne Park SE6 4XZ and Ravensbourne Park Crescent
Opening times: 8 am to sunset
Facilities: Seats, swings for children
Designation: Public park
Size: 0.8 hectares (2 acres)

Above: 60–62 Ravensbourne Park

Enjoying the park amongst the cow parsley and bluebells in May

St Margaret's Square

The Bridge House Estates is a charitable trust which was founded way back in 1282 to build and maintain London Bridge. It raised income from bridge tolls, taxes on goods transported over the bridges and taxes on properties along the river owned by the trust.

Today the trust continues to maintain London Bridge, Tower Bridge, Southwark Bridge, Blackfriars Bridge and the Millennium Bridge. The Estates also makes charitable donations from its surplus income through the City Bridge Trust.

Like many of the City Livery Companies the Trust invested in land. The Bridge House Estates owned farmland in Brockley in 1844 which was worked by James Houldsworth. But by the end of the 19th century the trust had replaced farmland with houses on Adelaide Avenue, St Margaret's Road and part of Brockley Road.

St Margaret's Square is a rectangular green space, slightly sunken, in front of Nos. 34–50 Adelaide Avenue. It was probably intended as a small garden to set off the houses and for the use of the residents, and originally the wall along the pavement was topped with railings.

Access: Adelaide Avenue SE4 1YX
Opening times: Always open
Facilities: None
Designation: Pocket Park
Size: 0.129 hectares (0.3 acres)

Wickham Gardens

Wickham Road of c.1850 is the widest of the roads in Brockley and the oldest. Wickham Gardens was originally a semi-circular garden surrounded by Victorian houses which were built in the 1880s. The houses on the north and west are original but those on the south and east sides of the green were destroyed by a V2 bomb in 1945 and replaced by flats in the 1960s. The area was under the bomber flight path to the London Docks which is why there was so much damage here during WWII.

The ornamental garden of 1928 was owned by Mr Alfred H Tarleton. A low wall still surrounds three side of the garden but the original iron railings on top of the wall have gone, as has the ornamental garden. Trees surround the green with parasol-shaped twiggy bushes around the perimeter. What a wonderfully attractive garden this could be!

Mews are very much a feature of Brockley and there is a delightful mews at the entrance to Wickham Gardens. Cranfield Mews is an unmade service road behind the houses and links Wickham Gardens to Harefield Road. It is paved with the original setts of paving stones and shaded by trees. This little passage, one of the prettiest of the mews, is quite hidden away and when you walk down the lane it feels as is you are in the countryside.

Access: Wickham Gardens SE4 1NA
Opening times: Always open
Facilities: None
Designation: Pocket Park
Size: 0.068 hectares (0.2 acres)

SOUTH AND SOUTH EAST LEWISHAM

Catford, Rushey Green, Hither Green and Southend only started developing in the late 1800s. Even after WWI the area of the Downham and Bellingham estates was countryside, offering rural walks and income from farming and market gardens. But WWI was a turning point for urban development and rural life in this corner of Lewisham rapidly disappeared.

Catford is variously described as a manor, an area of land, or just a crossing over the River Ravensbourne with a colony of wild cats! The earliest reference is to Catteford in 1240 and Catte is Anglo-Saxon for cat so perhaps the last explanation is credible. In the 18th century the manor came to Edward Eliot who was created Baron Eliot of St Germans in 1784 and Earl of St Germans in 1815. Catford as an independent district only dates from the late 1800s; the parish church was built in 1887 and Catford Railway Station dates from 1892.

Below: Catford Railway Station

Rushey Green was Russheteteslond in Old English, meaning a low-lying area with rushes. In 1863 it was a hamlet on both sides of the River Ravensbourne roughly covering the area of today's shopping centre in Catford. The manor house of Lewisham was thought to have been in Rushey Green.

Hither Green was once the site of a hamlet of the Manor of Romborough for which there are no records after the mid-1300s. Godfrey Smith suggests it was wiped out by the Black Death in the mid-14th century. Hither Green only appeared as a place name in the early 1700s and the centre of the hamlet, the green, is thought to have been near the gates of the former Hither Green Hospital on Hither Green Lane.

Hither meant near to the centre of Lewisham, while Further Green, another of several greens in Lewisham, was further away in the vicinity of Verdant Lane. The area was farmland and woodland but by the 18th century most of the trees had been cut down and country mansions were starting to appear. Mountsfield House, built in the 19th century was one of the country estates.

As in other parts of Lewisham it was the advent and spread of the railways which accelerated development.

From 1896 Archibald Cameron Corbett started building in Catford and Hither Green. He negotiated a deal for season tickets on the new railways and ensured the new Hither Green Station which opened in 1895 gave good access to the estate, thereby increasing the attraction of the houses to buyers. He also donated the land for St Andrew's Church (1903–04) but did not build pubs because he disapproved of alcohol!

Southend stood at the south end of Lewisham on the road to Bromley. In the 1800s it was still a small rural hamlet of a few houses and two pubs on the River Ravensbourne which serviced two significant mills in the hamlet.

In the 18th century the Lower Mill was where Ephraim How and his son produced high quality cutlery. By 1796 Mr Batley was producing mustard at the same mill. The mill pond is still in place as Southend Pond outside

Homebase on the Bromley Road. The Upper Mill nearby was always used for grinding the corn grown in the area.

Southend Hall was the big house here and stood at the corner of today's Whitefoot Lane and the Bromley Road. John Forster (1747–1834) acquired the land and the family lived here from the early 1800s. Southend was in the parish of St Mary's in Lewisham which involved a muddy tramp down the road to attend church, and so he also built a small chapel of ease in 1824. Today the chapel is used as the church hall for the adjacent Church of St John the Baptist for which the family contributed land and money. The new church serviced the rapidly expanding community and was consecrated in 1928.

By the early 1900s the Forsters owned c.1,000 acres of land in Lewisham and were very wealthy. The family left Southend Hall just before WWI for their home in Hampshire and the Hall was finally demolished in 1937 so that Whitefoot Lane could be widened and straightened.

Beringaham was one of the small manors within the Manor of Lewisham and there seems to be broad agreement that the name means land belonging to Beora's people. The name of Bellingham was adopted when the railway station opened in 1892. The manor house survived as Bellingham Farm which was only demolished in the 1930s.

The construction of the Downham Estate was a similar initiative to that of the Bellingham Estate. Land was compulsorily purchased and the development undertaken by the London County Council between 1924–30 after Lewisham Council had opposed the plans. The estate was built over the farms of Shroffolds (see Reigate Road Open Space) and Holloway (see Downham Playing Fields) which belonged to Lord Northbrook, a member of the Baring family, and the Lord of the Manor of Lee.

The estate of over 6,000 homes and c.400 flats was designed by George Topham Forrest and was named after Lord Downham, the Chairman of LCC 1919–20. The LCC tried to follow some of the garden city principles of Sir Ebenezer Howard but money was an issue and ambitions were scaled back. Nevertheless the estate seemed like 'paradise' to the new residents from poor inner-city areas.

Further reading:

Browning, Paul: www.runner500.wordpress.com
Coulter, John:
    Lewisham, History and Guide, 1994, Alan Sutton Publishing
Smith, Godfrey: *Hither Green, The Forgotten Hamlet*, 1997

St John's Church (left) and the chapel of ease (right) funded by the Forster family

Culverley Green

Culverley Green is a little triangular park between Culverley, Thornsbeach and Bargery Roads. It is recognised as one of the London Squares and it is perhaps a very early interpretation of a pocket park? Nevertheless, it is appreciated as a communal green space in an area of dense housing.

The housing here was developed by the Forster family on their Sangley Farm Estate between 1900–1920 in response to improved transport links with London: the railway network was expanding with new stations at Catford and Bellingham in 1892 and there were improvements to the network of horse-drawn trams in the 1890s, connecting Catford and Lewisham to the station in Greenwich.

James Watt was the main developer of the Sangley Farm Estate and also worked on the Corbett Estate. He may have built some of the houses around the green. The housing has interesting details such as stained glass windows, carved and moulded capitals and window surrounds, sash windows and solid wooden doors.

Sporting facilities in the vicinity of the new estate included the Jubilee Ground which was used as a first-class cricket ground by Kent County Cricket Club from 1875–1921, and the Catford Cricket and Lawn Tennis Club which was established in 1890 and whose pavilion still stands on Penerley Road.

Access: SE6 2JZ
Opening times: Open dawn to dusk
Facilities: Seats
Designation: Public open space
Size: 0.15 hectares
Culverley Green Residents Association: www.culverleygreen.org

Above: View inside the green
Below: Bug hotel

Houses overlooking Culverley Green

Bellingham Green

After WWI new housing estates developed rapidly in south east London. The 1919 Housing and Town Planning Act (the Addison Act) was spoken of as 'housing for heroes' and although one aim was to provide improved housing for soldiers' families the legislation also required town councils to address the inadequate housing and poor health of disadvantaged families. The legislation was significant because it made housing a national responsibility.

The Bellingham Estate was built by the London County Council in 1920–25 and was one of the new post-WWI housing estates. It was built on the site of Bellingham Farm and White House Farm and lies between the Rivers Pool and Ravensbourne. Bellingham Farm was situated on either side of the railway line, just south of Bellingham station on land owned by the Forster family, and the farm house was on the site of Allerford Road.

Several of the streets in the estate are named after mills on the River Ravensbourne, such as Grangemill and Fordmill. At the end of Broadmead Road a footbridge crosses the River Pool and excavations in 1969 showed this was the route of the Roman road, the Lewes Way, which also crossed Blythe Hill. Broadmead was one of the great fields in the mediaeval Manor of Lewisham.

The Estate of 2,700 houses was envisaged along Sir Ebenezer Howard's 'garden city' principles of 1898 with wide, tree-lined avenues, varied house designs with interesting brick and window details, front gardens, large allotments behind the blocks of houses, and little greens off the main roads which radiated out from a larger central green. A church was designed by Sir Charles Nicholson and built in 1925 but not completed, and a school, shops and playing fields were also provided for the new community.

Bellingham Green was completely renovated by Lewisham Council in 2001–2003 and today offers good exercise facilities for people of all ages and a delightful sensory garden which really needs Friends to help look after the plants. Sadly the Hamish Horsley Sunstone sculpture of 1985 in the middle of the green has disappeared.

It is easy to take trees for granted but the trees on the perimeter of the park are beautiful: large London plane trees, flowering ash trees, pedunculate oaks and a stately red oak create a calming circle around Bellingham Green.

Access: Bellingham Green SE6 3JB
Opening times: Always open
Facilities: Outdoor gym, multipurpose ball court, protected play area for children under seven, children's play area and hall, seats
Designation: Green Flag public park
Size: 0.9 hectares (2.2 acres)

Below: Bellingham Green children's play area

Bellingham Green in June

Durham Hill

Before the 1920s the countryside here was known as the Seven Fields and it was popular for weekend rambles. Even today this beautiful hillside is a place to walk and to be alone with your thoughts. There are views towards Beckenham Place Park and Crystal Palace and on a clear day you can see the Shard at London Bridge.

Durham Hill was also known as Downham Fields and it is the highest point of the surrounding Downham Estate. The steepness of the hill would have made construction difficult and so the hillside was left as a public open space. In 2007 the Downham Health and Leisure Centre was built at the highest point of the park, offering a wide range of exercise options as well as a library, NHS services and a cafe.

The hillside is neutral grassland with a rich mix of grass species and wonderfully named wildflowers such as yellow hawkbit, goat's-beard, cat's-ear, ragworts, bird's-foot trefoil and beaked hawk's-beard. And yellow agrimony, purple knapweed and white and pink clovers flower in the spring and summer. You will find a copse of white willows and crack willows, mature willow trees, hornbeams, lime trees, a line of stately poplars on the crest of the hill, beech trees and a few ornamental trees.

The joy of this site is its openness. Visit this beautiful place at any time of the year and just let the cobwebs blow away.

Access: Moorside BR1 5EP,
Churchdown BR1 5PT, Downham Way BR1 5NS
Opening times: Always open
Facilities: Playing fields on top of the hill,
futuristic climbing frame, seats
Designation: Public park, SINC of Borough Importance
Size: c.13 hectares (32 acres)

Below and opposite: Durham Hill in April

Downham Playing Fields

A soccer match on Downham Playing Fields

Downham Playing Fields in Lewisham was created during the development of the Downham Estate as a leisure facility and a century later it still fulfils that function.

The two fields are flat and open and the little Spring Brook, a tributary of the River Ravensbourne, meanders through the fields before joining the Ravensbourne via an underground culvert.

The Spring Brook divides both of the fields into a grassy area with playing fields, and a wilder and more natural and narrower section. The southern field below Glenbow Road has a Pavilion and a children's play area.

In 1999–2000 restoration work in the fields included lowering the river bank to allow for flooding along its course and this has encouraged natural vegetation and wildlife. Interesting and attractives trees shade the brook: willows, alders, limes, beeches, and Caucasian wingnut trees.

Wildflowers such as white gypsywort and meadowsweet, pink ragged robin and mauve willowherb colour the banks, and swathes of uncut grass suggest a rural meadow, creating a surprising and pleasant area in which to enjoy a walk.

And if you venture across Valeswood Road into the Borough of Bromley you can follow the Spring Brook through Shaftesbury Park and find the Downham and Bellingham Cricket Club which opened in 1931 to provide sporting opportunities for the workmen building the Downham Estate.

Access: Glenbow Road BR1 4RL, Downham Way, Downham Lane
Opening times: Dawn to dusk
Facilities: Six soccer pitches, Pavilion with changing rooms, children's play area
Designation: SINC of Borough Importance
Size: 1 hectare (2.5 acres)
Friends of Downham Playing Fields: www.facebook.com

Left: Caucasian wingnut tree
Below: Lime tree leaves and seeds

Above: Ash tree leaves
Left: Beech nuts

The Spring Brook in June

Downham Woodland Walk

Downham Woodland Walk zigzags for 1.5kms between the Bromley Road and Moorside and it is also part of the Green Chain Walk linking Beckenham Place Park to Grove Park Nature Reserve. Although not part of the designated Woodland Walk, the rows of trees continue along Shaw Road, and down Woodbank Road.

The OS map of 1863 shows the walk as field boundaries extending from the Bromley Road eastwards along the boundary of Southend Hall and its fields to Whitefoot Lane and Shroffolds Farm. When the Downham Estate was built the green lane was retained and the facility is valued by local people and safeguarded by the Friends of Downham Woodland Walk.

The walk is in four distinct sections which are all lined with mature pedunculate oak trees, ash, hornbeam, coppiced hazel and wild service trees. In the spring you will find bluebells and wood anemones which are good indicators of Ancient Woodland, and this means the site dates from at least 1600.

According to the Woodland Trust only 2.5% of the UK still has Ancient Woodland. However, it doesn't follow that the trees we see today are 400 years old, simply that the site has been wooded for perhaps that length of time. It also means the land has never been cleared of trees or ploughed and the trees have been able to renew themselves.

The widest and the most diverse section of the Walk is between Moorside Road and Downderry Road and it also has a remarkably calm atmosphere. Wildflowers include garlic mustard, lords and ladies, lesser celandine, wood anemone and herb Robert amongst others. People have reported greater spotted woodpeckers, bullfinches and willow warblers and there are squirrels and insects aplenty!

The Downham Woodland Walk is a delight at all times of the year.

Access: Moorside Road, Downderry Road, Haddington Road, Oakridge Road junction with the Bromley Road BR1 5QW
Opening times: 8 am to sunset
Facilities: Seats
Designation: Local Nature Reserve, SINC of Borough Importance Grade I
Size: 3.9 hectares (9.6 acres)
Friends of Downham Woodland Walk:
www.downhamwoodlandwalk.wordpress.com

Below: Wood anemones in April
Opposite: Downham Woodland Walk in early February

Forster Memorial Park

A century ago this park was farmland in the countryside outside Lewisham and the Forster family were the landowners. In 1919 Lord Forster gave an area of part woodland and part fields to the Borough Council for a public park in memory of his two sons, John and Alfred Henry, who both died in WWI. The park was officially opened in 1922 by one of their sisters, Mrs Dorothy Lubbock.

The main central field is covered in grass and used for sports. It is surrounded by Ancient Woodland with pedunculate oak trees, ash and hazels with signs of coppicing, and bluebells and wood anemones in the spring. The curving path through the woodland along Whitefoot Lane is the original line of the lane before the road was widened and straightened. An unexpected avenue of Scots pines hides away along the border with Conisborough College.

The three meadows have a wealth of wildflowers including cranesbill, dead nettle, ragged robin, cinquefoil, buttercups, garlic mustard, great willowherb and oxeye daisies and each have their own character. The meadow nearest Conisborough College was formerly a piggery and orchards and seems to be favoured by dog walkers. And the hillside of lawns and trees accessed from the most westerly gate on Whitefoot Lane is used by picnickers. The wildest part is the sloping meadow alongside Whitefoot Lane.

You are never alone in this varied and interesting park. As well as people there are numerous insects and birds, squirrels scamper about in the trees or undergrowth and ring-necked parakeets are always squeaking or gurgling somewhere.

Access: Whitefoot Lane, Longhill Road, and Bellingham Road.
Opening times: 8 am to sunset
Facilities: Basketball court, children's play area, football pitches on the central grassed area, cycle track, cafe, outside classroom for Forest School, table tennis table, all-weather cricket surface, toilets
Designation: Public park, SINC of Borough Importance
Size: 16.46 hectares (40.7 acres)
Friends of Forster Memorial Park: www.forsterparkfriends.org

Above: Ring-necked parakeets in the park
Opposite: The park in winter

Hither Green Cemetery

Francis Thorne designed Lee Cemetery with two Gothic chapels and winding paths among trees and he himself is buried here. The cemetery opened in 1873, a beautiful site on undulating ground which feels like a garden in which people are resting. Mature oak trees and spreading copper beeches line curving paths, with lime, holly and horse chestnut trees, and of course yew trees and conifers. And in autumn and early winter the graves are covered in a richly coloured blanket of leaves.

The original two Gothic-style chapels are still in place. The Anglican chapel, designed by Francis Thorne, is in good order, but the Dissenters' chapel for Methodists and Baptists, which also dates from 1873, was damaged during WWII and has been left to decay, which is a pity. It was designed by William Webster, an important building and engineering contractor in the 19th century, who lived in Wyberton House near St Margaret's Church in Lee and was buried in that churchyard.

Hither Green Cemetery, as the burial ground is known today, is now a vast cemetery of c.58 acres. The new areas are laid out in neat rows with few trees and apparently little interest in creating a garden to complement or continue the original design ideas.

The Commonwealth War Memorial in the new cemetery commemorates 241 service men and women killed in both world wars although some of the graves are placed elsewhere in the cemetery. It is always sad to find a Kipling stone, the standard headstone of a service man or woman killed in war, for a young person with the much later memorials of their parents.

On 20th January 1943 a Primary School on Sandhurst Road was bombed during WWII, killing 38 children and 6 of their teachers. They are remembered on a memorial wall around a mass grave near the Commonwealth War Graves Memorial. This is a very stark part of the cemetery, and perhaps that is appropriate.

Above: In the cemetery in early December

Ring-necked parakeets are an increasing feature of south east London and have made the poplar trees between the cemetery and the neighbouring crematorium a particularly special overnight home!

Access: Verdant Lane SE6 1JX
Opening times: 10 am to 4 pm or 5 pm depending on time of year, but closed for burials; check the Lewisham Borough Council website for closure times
Facilities: Toilets
Designation: SINC of Borough Importance
Size: 23.4 hectares (58 acres)

The Dissenters' chapel in the original part of Hither Green Cemetery in December

Left: The Anglican chapel
Above: The Taylor family mausoleum
Below: Leland Lewis Duncan's grave

The War Memorial and war graves with Kipling stones in the new cemetery in late April

Hither Green Crematorium

The crematorium dates from 1956 and it is laid out as a grassy park with a long, narrow water feature leading to a small lake. The water attracts birds and mallards and moorhens are able to nest safely on the small island in the lake where wetland plants such as willow weed and rushes soften the edges of the water.

The site is beautiful in its own, sad way.

Access: Verdant Lane SE6 1JX
Opening times: 10 am to 4 pm or 5 pm depending on time of year; closed for burials; Lewisham Borough Council website for opening times
Facilities: Toilets, seats
Designation: SINC of Borough Importance
Size: 23.4 hectares (58 acres)

Below: The parkland in the crematorium in early April
Opposite: The water feature and small lake

Hither Green Triangle Nature Reserve and Springbank Road Community Garden

The Southeastern Railway line was built through Hither Green in the 1860s, diverging to go to Sidcup and Orpington. Originally this was just a junction in the countryside but when housing started to spread Hither Green Station opened in June 1895.

The original entrance to the station was in Springbank Road and it was built to service the St Germans Estate. Today the Saravia Court block of flats is built on the site. Saravia was the original name for Springbank Road and commemorates Adrian de Saravia, a French refugee who was the Vicar of St Mary's Church in Lewisham from 1596–1610. The station master's house still stands at 69 Springbank Road and the redbrick gate posts into the flats are the original gate posts for the station.

The nature reserve is between platforms 4 and 5 of Hither Green Station and the Hither Green Triangle Group work with Nature Conservation Lewisham on a few days in the year to keep the vegetation under control in the area.

The tree cover is sycamore, oak, ash and wild cherry, and a mix of indigenous plants such as white wild carrot, common violet-purple vetch, common purple knapweed and yellow lady's bedstraw. The site supports birds, butterflies, beetles and foxes. A small stream at the eastern end of the site forms a pond which has been refurbished by the Hither Green Triangle Group.

The Hither Green Community Association is a separate association and a licensed community rail group,

Below: The Station Master's house and the original entrance to the station

Below: Dense vegetation in the nature reserve

Above: Ripening plums in the garden

Above: Japanese anemones in the garden in August

and its volunteers work hard to maintain the outer two railway embankments. The HGCA maintains the station wildflower meadow and plants native tree species each winter in the wild area on the Springbank Road and Fernbrook Road embankments.

The Springbank Road Community Garden has been developed from wasteland as a pocket park in front of the flats and was first planted in 2009 by volunteers from the Hither Green Community Association. The garden makes its own compost and harvests rain from the roof of the bus shelter, and even produces juicy plums! The HGCA also fund street trees and have gifted fruit trees to local schools and parks.

There is no access to the nature reserve and it is not open to the public. It is a SINC of Borough importance and covers 11.4 hectares (28 acres)

Springbank Road Community Garden is not open to the public but is clearly visible from the pavement and the bus stop at SE13 6SS

Mountsfield Park

Henry Stainton senior bought Nine Acre Field land and built Mountsfield House in 1845–47. It is said he gave it to his son, Henry Tibbats Stainton, as a wedding present. Henry Tibbats Stainton (1822–92) was a significant entomologist who co-authored *A Manual of British Butterflies and Moths*. In 1903 the Council bought 2.5 hectares of the property and the public park opened on 7 August 1905. The house was originally intended to be a library but was found to be unsafe and was instead demolished. Over the years the Council bought more land from the School Board for London and Trinity College and also incorporated the Charlton Athletic football ground at the bottom of the hill into the park. Originally the park offered an open-air theatre, drinking fountains and ponds, but these have all gone.

The trees in the park are glorious and they are particularly colourful in the autumn. There are mature pedunculate oak trees, knarled hawthorns, old London plane trees, willows, wonderful hornbeams and soaring poplar trees. The trees are mainly around the perimeter and they are particularly thick near the entrance from Ringstead Road where it feels like woodland.

The very large Community Garden near Stainton Road is well-used with lots of vegetables, fruit and fruit trees, and impressive compost heaps. But the adjacent formal garden looks incomplete. Is this the remains of the formal garden for Mountsfield House?

There is always someone jogging, walking or playing in the park, and there are plenty of benches for those who just want to relax with a coffee from the cafe.

Access: Stainton Road SE6 1AN, George Lane SE13 6RY, Brownhill Road SE6 2DN, Ringstead Road SE6 2BG
Opening times: 8 am to sunset
Facilities: Children's playground, playing fields, outdoor gym gear, tennis and ball courts, Cafe
Designation: Green Flag public park, SINC of Borough Importance
Size: 13.4 hectares (32 acres)
Friends of Mountsfield Park: www.mountsfieldpark.wordpress.com

Above: The bandstand on top of the hill
Below: Walking the dogs in the large playing fields on top of the hill

The oak trees near the site of Mountsfield House in November

Wisteria flowering in the formal gardens in May

View down the hill to the River Ravensbourne valley with One Tree Hill on the horizon

Reigate Road playground and embankment

There is a curious green space to the east of Hither Green Crematorium with a children's playground, an embankment, a path leading to a footbridge over the railway line, and a small field behind the houses on Reigate Road. The embankment was in preparation for the Ringway Road scheme, which was abandoned, and the footbridge over the railway leads to the Railway Children Walk and the Grove Park Nature Reserve.

John King suggests this was the site of Shroffold's Farm which was one of very large old farms in the area, and he is perhaps supported by the presence of damson trees behind the houses on Reigate Road. The farm was in the Manor of Lee which was owned by Sir Francis Baring, later the Baron Northbrook.

Three particularly interesting wildflowers for this part of Lewisham can be found on the embankment: viper's bugloss, wild marjoram and greater knapweed. These green spaces, the playground, the embankment and the open space behind the houses look like an interesting project waiting for the care and attention of local residents.

Access: Reigate Road
Opening times: Playground open 8 am to sunset; embankment and path always open
Facilities: Children's play area, seats
Designation: Playground and public open space, SINC Grade I
Size: 0.15 hectares (0.4 acres)

Below: The hidden side of the embankment in April

Below: The children's playground

The path alongside the embankment, with the little field behind the houses on Reigate Road on the left

THE RIVER RAVENSBOURNE AND THE RIVER POOL PARKS

The River Ravensbourne and its tributaries have shaped the physical landscape over thousands of years, carving out a river valley which has sheltered people and animals. The river has attracted settlement, supported farming and powered industry.

The Ravensbourne rises at Caesar's Well in Keston Ponds, south of Bromley and is c.17kms (11 miles) long, flowing through Bromley, Lewisham and Greenwich to join the Thames at Deptford Creek. The two main tributaries are the Quaggy to the east which joins the Ravensbourne at Confluence Park close to Lewisham Station, and the Pool to the west which runs through Bellingham and Southend and and joins the Ravensbourne at the confluence in Catford.

The catchment area of the river and its various tributaries is considerable — 180kms^2 — with 66kms of river and streams. The Ravensbourne Catchment Action Group was set up in 2012 and aims 'to improve the rivers and provide wider benefits for people and nature at a catchment scale'.[17]

There were eleven mills on the River Ravensbourne in Lewisham in 1086, according to the *Domesday* book, and four more in Greenwich.

By the early 14th century Leland L Duncan says there were still nine mills on the river but he may not be strictly accurate:[18]

Toddelesmill had various spellings and seems to have been two mills: one ground corn and the other, the Armoury Mills established by Henry VIII, produced fine armour until c.1640. The Armoury Mills were rebuilt in c.1800 and became a small-arms and munitions factory. In 1820 the mill and surrounding lands were bought by Robert Arnold who made thread from raw silk and from 1826 this was known as the Silk Mills. Later the mills produced gold and silver thread for military uniforms, becoming one of the leading manufacturers in the UK and in the process discovered how to make tinsel! Demand shrank after WWI; the buildings passed through several hands and were finally demolished in the 1970s–80s and all that remains are two gate posts.

- Semannes Mill was also known as Bridge Mill and belonged to the Bridge House Estate. It was probably the mill known as Riverdale Mill in today's Riverdale Sculpture Park.
- Slagraves Mill was at Ladywell where there was a Slagrove Farm, and it is remembered in today's Slagrove Close.
- Ford Mill was probably Catford Mill. Lawrence Beale Collins cites three mills at the confluence of the Pool and Ravensbourne Rivers: Ford Mill, Grange Mill and Catford Bridge Mill.
- Frere Mill (was this the same as Grange Mill?) was probably at Bellingham.
- Knappen Mill or Knappemill, Livinges Mill, and Shrafholte Mill might have been at Southend.
- And the location of Pumfretes Mill is not mentioned; could Duncan be confusing this with Pomfret Manor on the Isle of Dogs?

Duncan doesn't mention the Tide Mill which stood just north of Deptford Bridge and which can be traced to at least the 12th century.

The last working mill, Robinson's Flour Mill at Deptford Bridge, was only demolished in the 1970s. The stretch of the Ravensbourne from Deptford Bridge to the Thames is tidal and was always heavily industrialised with industries including saw mills, soap and candle manufacturers, potteries, and the manufacture of superphosphates and copperas or ferrous sulphate. Ferrous sulphate was used in the production of dyes, sulphuric acid and other industrial products. In the 19th century Ferranti's power station stood at the mouth of the river. The Ravensbourne powered industry, but it was also transported goods from the mills and factories to the River Thames. And it provided drinking water until the water became too polluted.

Floods have been recorded regularly along the Ravensbourne and its tributaries. Nathan Dews says a flood in 1824 'carried away the houses and warehouses on each side of the [Deptford] bridge, together with the tide mill below, and its embankments'.[19] In 1875 the *Evening Standard* reported floods in south east London where the Ravensbourne and Quaggy rose by four feet in fifteen minutes.

The mouth of Deptford Creek where the Ravensbourne flows into the Thames. Canary Wharf business centre on the Isle of Dogs lies beyond.

Barge in Deptford Creek at the Tideway Construction site, a reminder of the industrial past of the Ravensbourne in Deptford.

In 1878 the *South London Press* reported that all along Lee Road to Lewisham houses were flooded by the Quaggy. Leland L Duncan describes the area around Lee Bridge at the bottom of Belmont Hill where 'the whole of the roadway has been considerably raised to keep it above the level of the Quaggy'[20] which also flooded at Lee Green. In 1931 Thurston Road was under water from the Ravensbourne. The last major floods were in 1968 when the entire area from Catford to Loampit Vale was impassable because of flooding. Paul Browning covers these floods in considerable detail, with lots of photographs.[21] Less severe flooding occurred in 1972, 1992 and 1993.

The authorities' response to the disaster was to confine the river in concrete channels to move it more quickly downstream to a major outlet, in this case the River Thames. Now we believe the opposite and, where possible, the river is allowed to follow its natural course, with provision for flooding in water meadows (even if modest). This slows the flow of the water and prevents flooding from a buildup downstream. Natural flora and fauna return and flourish, creating opportunities for enjoyment and learning. The Quaggy Waterways Action Group (QWAG) has been very active and influential in challenging traditional wisdom and bringing about change, particularly along the Quaggy.

Today comfortable housing and creative communities line the river at Deptford Creek and there is very little indication of the poverty and heavy industrialisation of the past. Local people care about the health and appearance of their rivers and every year the '3 Rivers Clean Up' attracts volunteers in a three-week project to clear invasive species and pick up litter in the Ravensbourne, Quaggy, and Pool Rivers. Walkers and cyclists on the Waterlink Way, a track from the mouth of the River Ravensbourne to South Norwood Country Park, enjoy the increasing birdlife and flourishing wild flowers and riverside vegetation in their urban surroundings.

Further reading:

Macartney, Sylvia, and West, John: *The Lewisham Silk Mills*, 1982, Lewisham Local History Society
Philpott, Christopher: www.greenwichindustrialhistory.blogspot.com

Above: Mumford's Flour Mill at Deptford Bridge near the Broadway and at the head of the tidal Ravensbourne dates from c.1790 when it was built as a timber-framed building for grinding corn. The oriel window is at the top of the grain silo of 1897 by Aston Webb. The building was converted to flats in 2005.

Broadway Fields and Brookmill Park

The Broadway was the green in the centre of Deptford Upper Town which today has become the wide crossroads where Brookmill Road meets the A2. The name lives on as Broadway Fields.

On Stanford's map of 1862 Broadway Fields was still market gardens, but in 1932 the site opened as Deptford Municipal Playing Fields. The playing fields were redeveloped when the Docklands Light Railway (DLR) was laid down in 1996–99. The layout was changed, new sports facilities were built and new trees were planted but the river remained in a concrete channel. The residential flats on the north side of Broadway Fields are built on Seager Place, once the site of various breweries and distilleries at the Broadway.

From Broadway Fields a path leads along the river, past the Stephen Lawrence Centre to Brookmill Park. On the John Roque map of 1746 a water mill stood on the site of the centre. Could this be the mill which John Evelyn described in his *Diary*? '28th April, 1668. To London, about the purchase of Ravensbourne Mills, and land around it, in Upper Deptford, of one Mr. Becher'. By the 1850s the mill was subsumed into the water extraction company.

There were two mills on this stretch of the River Ravensbourne: the corn mill which John Evelyn bought, and the Armoury Mill which was to the east of today's Elverson Road DLR station and which had been on the site since the 14th century.

The river serviced industries but it also provided water for domestic consumption and the Ravensbourne Waterworks was founded in 1701 to supply Woolwich, Greenwich and Deptford. In 1805 it was bought by the Kent Water Works Company. As the water in the river became more polluted through increasing industrialisation water for domestic consumption was extracted from wells on the site instead. After further changes in ownership the Metropolitan Water Board took over the water supply in 1902. Today the only evidence of waterworks is the James Engine House on the opposite side of the river and the small pond in the park, the remains of the reservoir for the pumping station.

Brookmill Park has been redesigned several times. After WWII the park reopened in 1951 as Ravensbourne Park, the name still displayed on the main gate, but in 1965 the name reverted to Brookmill Park. Major changes came again in 1999 when the DLR was built to connect Lewisham to the City. The course of the river was moved in both parks and in Brookmill Park much of the concrete channel was removed to create small flood plains. A nature reserve (closed to the public) was set aside on the north bank of the river, near the footbridge at Elverson Road station. The station is named after elvers, which are young eels, and eels can still be found in the river.

The Friends undertake regular river cleanups, they organise arts activities for families and the gardening group helps to maintain the formal garden. Their website carries a useful map to the park.

Brookmill Park is a much-loved green space in the centre of Lewisham with some wonderful trees. The mature London plane tree near the playground is believed to be around 300 years old, and nearby is a huge copper beech tree of perhaps 150 years to admire.

Walk along the river at any time of the day or just sit and watch it meander along. The ring-necked parakeets squeak overhead and numerous other birds can be found on the pond, creating an exceptional variety of birdlife which delights serious birdwatchers. And if you sit quietly you will almost certainly have a heron or a white egret for company and you may even see the blue flash of the kingfisher.

Access: Brookmill Road SE8 4HY, Deptford Bridge and Elverson Road DLR stations
Opening times: Always open
Facilities: Multipurpose ball court, children's play area, seating, cycle track and footpath on The Waterlink Way
Designation: Metropolitan Open Land, Brookmill Park is a SINC of Borough Importance and Green Flag public park
Size: 4.5 hectares (11 acres)
Friends of Brookmill Park: www.brookmillpark.deptfordcreek.net

Above: Broadway Fields from Brookmill Road
Below: The DLR runs on one side of Broadway Fields, across the river

Below: The River Ravensbourne is culverted in Broadway Fields

Above: The fountain and formal garden in Brookmill Park in summer
Below: Roses in the formal garden in June

Above: The James Engine House, the DLR and the river in winter
Below: One of the herons in the pond

The Ravensbourne in early January

Brookmill Road Nature Reserve

The original railway line from Nunhead to Blackheath Hill Station opened in 1871 and it was extended to Greenwich Park in 1888. The stations on the line were Nunhead, Brockley Lane (a few yards away from today's Brockley Station), Lewisham Road (one former booking office is part of a salvage yard, the other has been converted to a house), Blackheath Hill (between Sparta Street and Blackheath Hill) and Greenwich Park (where today's Ibis Hotel stands). The line closed during WWI and a short section of disused railway embankment forms today's small nature reserve.

In 1979 the Borough Council bought the land from British Rail and a nature reserve was developed with the help of the London Wildlife Trust. Today it is managed by the Nature Conservation Department of Lewisham Borough Council.

Another short section of the embankment can be seen in Brookmill Park, on the opposite side of Brookmill Road, and this is managed as a 'wild' area of the park.

Hornbeam and hazel trees have replaced a preponderance of sycamore trees and recently new paths have been laid. Steps and railings lead to the top of the very steep embankment where there is a small, circular glade with seating for learners during teaching sessions.

Cow parsley and bluebells tumble down the sides of the embankment and it is a delight to walk along the path, and up and over the top of the embankment, hidden from the world rushing past in trains and cars.

Access: Brookmill Road SE8 4JJ
Opening times: Not open to the general public; access via the Borough Conservation Office which organises work days and school visits
Facilities: None
Designation: Local Nature Reserve, SINC of local importance
Size: 0.43 hectares (1 acre)
Brookmill Road Nature Reserve: www.lewisham. gov.uk/inmyarea/openspaces/nature-reserves

Above: The steps up and over the railway embankment
Below: Heather Burrell's gates into the reserve

The path through the reserve under the slope of the railway embankment

Confluence Park

This tiny park is a new and imaginative opening-up of the confluence of the Rivers Quaggy and Ravensbourne near Lewisham Station as part of the Lewisham Gateway development. Yes, it is very small but a heron and a white egret visit regularly and the space offers a few minutes of nature before catching a train or shopping.

In the early 19th century the site would have looked very different indeed. The Plough Inn stood approximately on the site of the new Brick Kiln One residential flats. The inn overlooked Plough Green and the Plough Bridge which crossed the River Quaggy where the road crosses the river today, outside the new Premier Inn, just north of St Stephen's Church. Beyond The Plough Inn stood H & V Nicholl's Anchor Brewery, on the site of today's Tesco Supermarket. The office for the brewery, Eagle House of 1870, still stands in the supermarket car park and the name lives on in The Anchor pub at the bottom of Lewisham Hill.

The Quaggy seems to have had two arms joining the Ravensbourne here; the northern arm is in today's Confluence Park, and another arm to the south is perhaps under the road today? Inbetween was 'farmland, corn and pasture, with the well-wooded rising ground of Belmont and The Cedars in the rear'.[22] The Roebuck Inn, 'a picturesque wooden house',[23] was a second pub on the green until the mid-1850s, roughly on the site of the Church of St Stephen which was consecrated in 1865.

With rivers, gardens, pubs and good fishing this must have been a very pretty area in the early 1800s, and a very busy river crossing.

Today we have the Lewisham Gateway tower blocks instead of attractive country inns, a pocket park instead of the green and farmland, and busy shoppers and commuters instead of anglers, but at least we can see the rivers again.

Access: Lewisham railway station and Lewisham High Street
Opening times: Always open
Facilities: Seats
Designation: Pocket park

Above: The former office of the Anchor Brewery in the Tesco supermarket car park
Opposite: Confluence Park

Cornmill Gardens and Riverdale Sculpture Park

Lewisham Bridge Mill was a mediaeval corn mill which stood on Sundermead, common land of c.17 acres on the west side of the Ravensbourne in the centre of Lewisham.

In 1756 Thomas Betts bought the mill and converted it for cutting glass, the first site in London to use water-driven power for this purpose. He was a significant glass cutter and a very successful businessman, with a substantial factory in Lewisham which supplied his Kings Arms Glass Shop in Pall Mall. This explains the name The Glass Mills Leisure Centre. Jonathan Collett continued the business after Betts' death, but eventually the mill returned to grinding corn; it was rebuilt in the 1850s, closed in 1920, and was finally demolished in 1934.

In the 1960s the Sundermead Estate of council houses was built on the site, but by the turn of the century it had been decided to redevelop the centre of Lewisham. New blocks of flats with Italian names such as Sienna Alto and Venice Corte have replaced the Sundermead Estate. The names have no obvious historical connection to Lewisham and part of the history of this area is probably lost.

However, a small new park opened in 2007 and in 2009 the park received the Best New Public Space Award at the London Planning Awards, and a Green Flag Award in 2020, one of fifteen in Lewisham.

A small section of the river has been taken out of the culverts and the banks regraded. Riverside planting includes indigenous plants and trees (rushes, birch, alder, sweet gum) and the planting is slowly starting to thicken and develop. Mallards, coots and moorhens potter up and down the river but are careful to keep out of the way when the river floods. The Ravensbourne in flood is an impressive sight!

Left:
The playground in Cornmill Gardens

The River Ravensbourne in Cornmill Gardens in winter

Close by is Riverdale Sculpture Park, the site of the Riverdale Mill. Leland Duncan suggests this was Semannesmill or Seemanysmille dating from the time of the *Domesday Book*. It is quite extraordinary to find the site of a mill which has existed for nearly one thousand years in the centre of Lewisham!

Tanning and the production of leather was an important industry in Lewisham in the 17th century. Skins were dried in the area around the Lewisham Bridge Mill and leather was made at the Riverdale Mill which is called a leather mill on Rocque's map of 1745.

The mill was rebuilt c.1830, probably by John Penn Senior who ran a major engineering business in Lewisham and Deptford which was further developed by his sons. By the end of the 1800s the site housed the John Wallis Flour Mill and finally in 1978 the adjacent Riverdale Bakery was demolished. The mill was redeveloped as residential flats in 2016. A 20th century water wheel stands next to the engine house, and the mill pond is in front of the building, hidden behind trees and shrubs.

In the small grassy area in front of the mill on Molesworth Street there is a column sculpture by John Maine, one of the pieces of public art commissioned by the Council in 2000. But the interesting area is on the west bank of the river where there are coppiced hazels, and the far side of the railway which is inaccessible and which has been allowed to remain wild.

Access: Loampit Vale and Molesworth Street
Opening times: Always open
Facilities: Children's play area, seats
Designation: Public parks; Cornmill Gardens is a SINC of Local Importance
Size: 1.3 hectares and 0.4 hectares

Above: A replica water wheel alongside The Mill House

The Mill House and the remains of the mill pond

Ladywell Fields

Ladywell Fields is a vast green space in the centre of Lewisham, nearly one mile long. These ancient water meadows along the River Ravensbourne have been documented for over 1,000 years as meadows and farmland.

The London County Council and the Lewisham Board of Works bought land here in 1889 to develop the Ladywell Recreation Ground for the expanding urban community and created a remarkable resource in what has become a busy inner-city suburb.

The park covers three fields and there are two railway lines through the park which are interesting rather than disturbing. The Mid Kent and North Kent Line through Ladywell Station (a Grade II listed building) to Catford Bridge Station runs through all three fields and opened in 1857. The line on the edge of the small, hidden area near Ladywell Lodge and through the most southerly field was built by the London, Dover and Chatham Company and is routed to Catford Station which opened in 1892.

The Ravensbourne flows on one side of the north field which is a wide water meadow where the project to open up the River Ravensbourne in 2008 as part of QUERCUS, with EU funding, is perhaps most obvious. An additional stream meanders through the middle of the field, with pools and riffles, and indigenous waterside plants and grasses soften the banks. A little nature reserve, cared for by a local school, hides away near the enormous spiral stair bridge over the railway into the middle field.

The middle field is bisected by the river. The Waterlink Way along its east bank is a well-used footpath and cycle path into the centre of Lewisham, or alternatively there is a path in the opposite direction through blocks of flats which replaced the Catford Greyhound Stadium into the centre of Catford.

The real joy is to step off the path and sit down on a bench at the river edge, or cross the Ravensbourne into the hidden, western side of the middle field and find Ladywell Lodge and another quiet path through the trees on a little backwater. Do this, and you may feel that you are in a little country village.

The Waterlink Way passes under a high railway bridge into the south field which is large, almost rectangular open parkland with the Ravensbourne flowing quietly on one side at the bottom of the hill. Sports fields are hidden away on the far side of the river.

The trees in Ladywell Fields are glorious. There are beautiful old London plane trees and mature pedunculate oak trees, a Dutch elm (one of the Great Trees of London), Monterey pine, birch trees, black poplars, mimosas, cherry trees, acers, willows (of course), Caucasian wingnut and ash trees. And finally in 2011 the Friends planted apples, pears, cherries and plums in a new community orchard in the south field. Like many of the parks in Lewisham, Ladywell Fields has an active and knowledgeable Friends Group and they have produced a useful guide to the trees in the park.

The park is crammed with good sports and playground facilities, but perhaps more importantly it is a beautiful and varied open space for walking and exploring, and just 'being'.

Access: Ladywell Road and railway station, and Catford Bridge railway station, Ravensbourne Park and Malyons Road, and several other small entrances
Opening times: Always open
Facilities: Tennis courts, bowling green, ball courts, skate park, children's playgrounds, adventure playground, outdoor gym gear, seats, cafe, cycle and walking route as part of the Waterlink Way, and the Ladywell Arena.
Designation: Green Flag Public Park, SINC of Borough Importance
Size: 21.5 hectares (53 acres)
Friends of Ladywell Fields: www.ladywellfields.blogspot.com

The north field of Ladywell Fields in October with its meandering little stream

The middle field of Ladywell Fields with the Waterlink Way on the left

Mature pedunculate oak trees in the south field of Ladywell Fields

Iona Close Orchard

Iona Close Orchard is a small nature reserve and an area of wildness 500 yards away from the South Circular Road in London. The site was rescued in 2012–13 and is now part-owned by London & Quadrant Housing Association and the Council and managed by Lewisham Council and the Friends of Ladywell Fields.

Once this was the gardens of the villas at 60–62 Ravensbourne Park which are Grade II listed homes built in 1825–30. What might the gardens have looked like at that time? The OS map of 1870 shows houses on Ravensbourne Park with geometrically laid out gardens and this would accord with the writings of John Claudius Loudon (1783–1843). He was a very influential garden designer and writer in his time and he advocated formal layouts for town gardens with detailed plans for gardens presented in his book *The Suburban Gardener and Villa Companion*.

The Friends found several old fruit trees when they started to clear the space including an old black mulberry tree and some pear trees. Several heritage fruit trees have been planted with support from The Orchard Project. And there are some brick setts at the bottom of the garden, but otherwise there are no clues to the former layout of the gardens.

Access and Opening times: Not open to the public
Facilities: None
Designation: SINC of Local Importance
Size: 0.4 hectares (1 acre)
Friends of Ladywell Fields: www.ladywellfields.blogspot.com

Above: Bluebells in Iona Close Orchard in spring

Looking up the hill and through the orchard towards the houses on Ravensbourne Park

Southend Pond and Peter Pan's Park

The Ravensbourne passes under Catford Bridge, where, yes, there was another mill, Catford Mill. The OS map of 1863 clearly shows a corn mill with a diversion in the river to create a mill stream. The mill seems to have been where Wickes stands today on the A205 Catford Road. This is the beginning of the Riverview Linear Park which follows the Ravensbourne for a few hundred yards before branching off along the River Pool from the confluence. From this point the Ravensbourne is hidden behind houses until Southend Pond.

The Lower Mill stood at the junction of Southend Lane and the Bromley Road and the pond alongside Homebase was its mill pond. This was where Ephraim How (1652–1729) and his son John produced beautiful and expensive cutlery in the early 18th century. The business flourished. The Hows standardised their designs, employed a lot of people at the mill in Southend, and sold their products in their shop in Clerkenwell. The quality and reputation of the cutlery was such that the name and the mark were frequently copied illegally. Ephraim How eventually became the Master of the Worshipful Company of Cutlers and his grave is in St Mary's Church in Lewisham.

After their time the mill was used for grinding mustard, and then reverted to its original purpose of grinding corn which continued until WWI. In the early 20th century the pond was even used for pleasure boating.

In 1922 the pond and surrounding area opened as 'a children's pleasureland' and included a boating lake, gardens, a small fun fair, sandpit and play park. JM Barrie agreed that the site could be named after his famous character on condition that any profits were donated to the Great Ormond Street Hospital.

Today the pond is crowded with Canada geese, mallards and coots; there are at least six turtles, and a number of very large fish. In the spring and summer the Canada geese march their new families across the busy Bromley road to the grass in front of the Church of St John the Baptist. The traffic stops, twice a day, and everyone smiles as the youngsters scamper and later waddle to lunch or back home to swim.

Above: *The Whisper* commissioned from André Wallace in 1981 on the island in Southend Pond
Right: Southend Pond

The name of the pleasureland lives on in Peter Pan's Park across the road from Southend Pond. The park was just a piece of wasteland until Phoenix Community Housing decided to create a public amenity with the help of local residents and volunteers. Mulalley donated their design services and the park opened in 2014.

A small stretch of the River Ravensbourne runs through the park which lies between the former Lower and Upper Mills. The Upper Mill stood on the eastern side of Beckenham Hill Road, next to Peter Pan's Park and on roughly the site of Ansford Road. There were two mill ponds on the bend of the Bromley Road as it turns south and the mill was used for grinding corn grown on local farms, but nothing remains of the building today.

The park is a pretty stretch of river shaded by large maple, sycamore, ash and beech trees with seats which encourage you to linger, and it manages to retain a feeling of calm, despite the nearby traffic.

Access: Junction of Bromley Road and Beckenham Hill Road
Opening times: Always open
Facilities: Seats
Designation: Public pocket park, SINC of Local Importance
Size: c.1 hectare (2.4 acres)

Above: The Chapel of Ease built by the Forster family in 1824 with the families of Canada Geese
Below: Tench in Southend Pond

Below: One of the turtles in Southend Pond

The Ravensbourne in Peter Pan's Park

Beckenham Place Park

Beckenham Place Park is the largest green space in the London Borough of Lewisham and a stately and gracious park which is beautiful at all times of the year. The Park has been described as 'probably the best single wildlife site in the Borough … the most extensive ancient woodlands in Lewisham, the most diverse acid grassland, the most natural stretch of river, [and] probably the oldest pond and the only willow carr'.[24]

The River Ravensbourne is at the eastern end of the park alongside two large fields. In 1863 the river flowed through reed beds in the northerly field. Today the reed beds have gone and the wide grassy space is known as The Common. A gate and a hedge of willow trees separate The Common from Summerhouse Fields, the second field, to the south of The Common.

In these fields we can enjoy the 'natural' River Ravensbourne in its floodplain. When the river reaches Foxgrove Road which is the most southerly point of the park the Ravensbourne is outside the Borough of Lewisham.

But the River Ravensbourne is only a small part of the story of Beckenham Place Park.

John Cator, a wealthy timber merchant and Member of Parliament, bought part of the Manor of Foxgrove in c.1760 and developed the property known as Stumps Hill as his country seat. The mansion was built in 1760–62 and is now Grade II* listed. In 1785 he moved the Beckenham Hill Road further north to enjoy greater privacy for the mansion. The lake was probably dug about the same time. His nephew, John Cator, inherited the property in 1806 on his uncle's death and added the portico to the house, as well as undertaking further work in the grounds. From 1815–1933 the mansion was tenanted, with a complicated history detailed on the Friends' website.

Then, in 1927 the London County Council bought the property from the Cator Estate and it opened as a public park two years later. In 1933 the first public golf course was opened here, but this was closed in 2017.

The Friends of Beckenham Place Park publish a very good map of the park with a circular walk showing points of interest.

The park's website has another good map and considering the size of the park it is good to have a map on your first visit.

The areas of ancient woodland which were once part of the Great North Wood are Summerhouse Hill Wood and Stumpshill Wood where there are towering pedunculate and sessile oaks, horse chestnuts and sweet chestnuts, ash and beech trees. The Woodland Trust has recorded c.eighteen Notable trees and c.eleven Veteran trees of all kinds in the park. And underneath the trees are the plants of ancient woodlands: bluebells, Solomon's seal and the native male fern.

Below: The Common alongside the river

The Ravensbourne in Beckenham Place Park in April

Stumpshill Pond on the edge of Stumpshill Wood is probably the oldest natural pond in Lewisham, although the origin of the pond is unclear. It is surrounded by willow carr which is wet woodland, generally alder or willow trees, in woods which are marshy or which flood regularly. There is more wet woodland just to the east of the swimming lake, on the site of the original lake.

It is thought the open parkland in front of the mansion was managed as wood-pasture, which means it was grazing land for cattle with pollarded oak and chestnut trees, i.e. the trees were pruned so that new growth occurred beyond the reach of the cattle or deer. This was common practice in the 19th century.

John Cator's father-in-law was Peter Collinson. Collinson was a cloth merchant but his real love was botany and he corresponded with a number of scientists and botanists in the UK and abroad, particularly John Bartram in North America from whom he imported seeds and plants. Collinson wrote to John Bartram in 1761: 'My son-in-law has built a large fine house and has everything to plant. Prithee send a box of your more rare trees for I have none to spare of rhododendrons, kalmias, small magnolias, azaleas and sassafras'.[25] There are still rhododendrons to be found but none of the other plants of any age.

The Green Chain Walk and the Capital Ring run through the park. The original lake has gone, although the depression is still visible on the ground. Instead, a swimming lake was created on part of the original lake in July 2019 and offers popular outdoor swimming.

This is a glorious park in which to wander at any time of the year.

Access: Various entrances from Beckenham Hill Road and Foxgrove Road
Opening times: The grounds are always open
Facilities: Cafe, Sunday Farmers Market, swimming lake, children's play area, paying car park
Designation: Public park, SINC of Metropolitan Importance
Size: 98 hectares (242 acres)
Friends of Beckenham Place Park: www.beckenhamplaceparkfriends.org.uk

Above: The swimming lake on the site of the original lake
Below: The sensory wldlife garden managed by the Friends

The mansion at Beckenham Place Park from Summerhouse Wood

This page: Summerhouse Wood in spring with old trees, bluebells, and fungi

One of the Notable pedunculate oak trees in the grounds of Beckenham Place Park

The Riverview Walk

The River Pool rises in South Norwood Country Park and flows northwards c.5.1kms (c.3 miles) to join the Ravensbourne at the confluence in Catford. It flows in a floodplain and one of the springs which feeds the river comes from Sydenham Wells Park, debouching near the supermarket at Bell Green. The Riverview Walk follows the River Pool from Southend Lane to Catford Bridge Station and it is a substantial section of the Waterlink Way.

People enjoy this lovely route in different ways — cycling, walking, just sitting, or, if you are a child, romping in the play park opposite the Winsford Road Bridge. It is particularly useful during the winter because the path is paved while the surrounding woods or grassy areas can be extremely muddy and slippery.

From Southend Lane to the Winsford Road Bridge the river meanders along a shallow valley, with the Bellingham Estate on the right. The river is canalised in places but grasses such as pendulous sedge, reed canary grass and reed sweet-grass in planters or on the riverbank soften the landscape. A small pond with large boulders and riffles has been created in the river near the Bellingham play park and nearby is a little wetland area with reeds, willows and alders, and wildflowers in the surrounding meadow.

The Winsford Road Bridge to the confluence is the quietest section of the walk, with the River Pool on one side and the railway line and the Bellingham Estate on the other. The river is less canalised and in some places a path runs along the water. This is more enjoyable in drier weather as it is narrow and can be very slippery. Flag irises, willowherb and marsh marigolds glow in the shade under willows, alder and ash trees and Indian balsam is pretty but invasive. Butterflies flutter in the meadows, foxes are common, and a variety of birds provide background music.

The short stretch from the confluence bridge, through the Wickes and Halfords Industrial Estate takes you under the road to Catford Bridge Station. At this point, if you need a longer walk, you can continue along the River Ravensbourne in Ladywell Fields.

The Riverview Walk in SE London is a quiet and peaceful walk along the River Pool which has been beautifully landscaped in recent years and it really feels as though you are walking in the countryside — a marvellous green space in Lewisham.

Access: Southend Lane SE26 5BH or
Catford Bridge Station SE6 4RE
Opening times: Always open
Facilities: Children's play area opposite Broadway Bridge
Designation: SINC of Borough Importance
Size: c.18 hectares (c.45 acres)
Friends of the River Pool: www.facebook.com

Below: Ma mallard taking the kids for a walk!
Opposite: River Pool in June

Above: Riffles and pools on the river to break the flow
Below: Chatting at the confluence

Top: Oxeye daisies

Centre: Buttercups

Bottom: Flag iris

The Waterlink Way alongside the River Pool which is hidden in the trees on the right

Wild Cat Wilderness

The Wild Cat Wilderness invites you to 'Join us this summer for all things wild! We have events and activities for all ages including volunteering, forest school sessions, cooking, learning about nature, arts and crafts, and fruit picking!' It is all about enjoying the outdoors in a safe environment.

In the 1600s, this part of Lewisham was land owned by the Leathersellers' Company. A survey of the Company's lands in 1793 included '3 fields called Long Meadows and Rushey Mead, adjoining Pool River, Sydenham'.[26] Long Meadow covered 11 acres in 1630 and today the allotments adjoining the site are listed as Long Meadows Allotments. This must indicate the Leathersellers' estate which stretched from the River Pool to the foot of Sydenham Hill. The Rev Abraham Colfe also bought land here to endow his charities which included Colfe's Grammar School. He appointed the Leathersellers' Company as his Trustees, increasing the Company's extensive control of land in Sydenham and Lewisham.

The site was once part of the allotments which stretch along the River Pool to the north, but became neglected and overgrown, and it is now being restored by volunteers.

The Wild Cat Wilderness is a charity and a community green space managed by the Rushey Green Time Bank for the community.

This is a FUN PLACE!

Access: Riverview Park SE6 4PL
Opening times: Check the website for opening times
Facilities: Outdoor kitchen, greenhouse, toilet, outdoor classroom
Designation: Community green space
Size: 2 hectares (5 acres)
Website: www.wildcatwilderness.org

Above: Maria in the vegetable garden with volunteers
Below: Apples ripening nicely in July

Above: Basecamp
Below: Wild Cat Wilderness apiaries

Above: An old pear tree house
Below: The outdoor kitchen

213

WEST AND SOUTH WEST LEWISHAM

In this part of Lewisham we find Sydenham and Forest Hill.

There are historical references to a Manor of Sippenham but this may have meant a large estate rather than a manor with judicial or fiduciary rights.

The Manor House was Place House which was built in 1580 for the Earl of Sussex and stood on the road from Lewisham to Bell Green, on the site of today's Creeland Grove. Apart from that, until the beginning of the 17th century Sydenham was a very small and remote country village around today's Bell Green with no direct road to London. There were a few large houses, farms in the low-lying areas, and the large open area of Westwood Common, an early name for Sydenham Common, lying on the hillside to the west.

The Great North Wood which used to cover the hills here started to disappear with the expansion of England's navy in the 16th century. The wood was transported down the old road through Brockley to the dockyards in Deptford and by the beginning of the 17th century most of the large oak trees on the common land had gone. The wood was what C J Schüler[27] calls a 'tree farm' which produced wood for various purposes using tree management techniques such as pollarding and coppicing, and most importantly the wood produced income for its owners. Commoners nevertheless had the right to graze their pigs and poultry on fallen acorns under the trees.

After c.1750 a few large mansions were built along Sydenham Road (the road from Bell Green westwards) such as The Lawn, Hanover Lodge and Whagow House but the journey into London was by coach and expensive, discouraging the development of middle-class housing.

In 1786 Mayow Wynell Mayow, a lawyer, bought the Old House Estate in Sydenham and by the end of the 1800s the family estate had expanded to include most of the land between Sydenham Road and Perry Vale, i.e. the area between today's Sydenham Station and Forest Hill Station. The area to the west of the Old House Estate, from Westwood Hill just under the ridge of hills and up to today's Forest Hill Station, was Sydenham Common. His grandson, Mayow Wynell Adams, remembers the common was 'covered with furze and fern, with patches of grass here and there', a place of 'pristine beauty and wildness'.

There were four events which changed Sydenham from countryside to town: Sydenham Common was enclosed between 1810–19; the land became available for speculative building; the Croydon to Brighton railway was built in 1836–39 along the line of the defunct Croydon Canal; and the Crystal Palace opened in 1854.

Sydenham Common, as common land, could be used by everyone living in the area for wood or to graze animals. The Rev Abraham Colfe led a successful campaign to stop the enclosure of Sydenham Common in the 17th century but in 1810 the Enclosure Act finally removed these rights. The Act was promoted by wealthy landowners in the area and 500 acres of common land was allocated to existing landowners: the Earl of Dartmouth who owned land in Blackheath and Lewisham; John Forster, who lived at Southend Hall (and whose descendant Lord Forster donated land for the Forster Memorial Park); the Earl of St Germans, and Mayow Wynell Adams. And once the land was enclosed it could be developed for housing.

Sydenham is divided into two by the railway line. Upper Sydenham rises up the hill to the west, and Lower Sydenham is on the lower slopes towards Bell Green in the east. The railway line from London Bridge to Croydon and Brighton was built in 1836–39 and offered speedy and affordable travel into London for business people. The new landowners and speculative builders could now target this middle-class market with their housing developments.

The Great Exhibition of 1851 in Hyde Park in central London aimed to educate people about the technological developments of the Industrial Revolution and rivalled the Paris Exhibition of 1849. It was housed in the Crystal Palace which was designed by Joseph Paxton and masterminded by Prince Albert as President of the Royal Society of Arts. When the exhibition closed the building was reconstructed in a different configuration on Penge Place Estate in Sydenham. The new Crystal Palace opened in 1854 as a major leisure and cultural attraction in London with regular exhibitions and ground-breaking musical concerts. The building stood in formal terraced gardens with the new feature of carpet bedding — swathes of brightly coloured flowers which proved very popular with the public and was soon copied elsewhere. And 'From the terrace in front of the palace a prospect is obtained of surpassing beauty over richly wooded and undulating plains to the distant hills of Kent and Surrey'.[28]

The Crystal Palace attracted affluent and influential residents who built themselves substantial new homes in large grounds in Upper Sydenham. In the first half of the 1800s the high street of Upper Sydenham was along Kirkdale, from Wells Park Road to Fransfield Grove and along Dartmouth Road. As housing developed the shopping centre moved down the hill to Cobb's Corner.

However, like many leisure attractions, the Crystal Palace needed to offer novelty and up-to-date facilities to attract visitors and when this didn't happen financial difficulties ensued. And then the building burned down in 1936.

By the end of the 19th century the structure of society and people's expectations were changing and after WWI the pressure to build new, smaller and cheaper homes or homes for rental was irresistible. Large mansions were sold to become institutions, or demolished and replaced with terraced housing or council estates. Sydenham and Forest Hill were absorbed into Greater London and countryside, woods and canals disappeared. In the words of Sir Walter Besant: the 'pathetic survival of the beautiful woods that crowned the steep hills of Norwood, Penge, and Sydenham, reminds one again of the wanton destruction of natural beauty which the indifference of Londoners has sanctioned until too late'.[29]

'Forest Hill' describes the state of the wooded countryside to the north of Sydenham Common until the end of the 1700s. In the time of Henry VIII this was common land but that right was ignored and the land was bought and sold as an investment over the centuries. The area had various names including Coulton's Wood or Coleson's Coppice and it was regarded as part of Sydenham.

The area was developed in response to the same events which changed Sydenham in the 19th century. The first houses were built along Honor Oak Road and by the mid-1800s the area was referred to as Forest Hill and separate from Sydenham. Similar to Sydenham this was an area where the first new housing was for the more affluent who wanted a rural lifestyle and could afford the cost of travel into London.

In Forest Hill the Dartmouth Park Estate was built with the impressive Christ Church Chapel as its centrepiece but sadly half the building is now residential and the graveyard is partly private and partly a school play area and closed during the week. Other sites in Forest Hill are the Horniman Museum and Horniman Nature Trail, the Horniman Triangle, Eliot Bank, One Tree Hill and, oddly, Sydenham Garden and associated sites. Sydenham sites carry an SE26 postcode while Forest Hill is identified by an SE23 postcode.

Further reading

Adams, Mayow Wynell: *Sydenham*, 1878; a British Library publication, printed by Amazon

Alcock, Joan P: *Sydenham and Forest Hill*, 2005, The History Press

Coulter, John: *Sydenham and Forest Hill Past*, 1999, Historical Publications

Grindlay, Steve: *Sydenham & Forest Hill Through Time*, 2014, Amberley Publishing

Spurgeon, Darrell: *Discover Sydenham and Catford*, 1999, Greenwich Guide-Books

Baxter Field and Kirkdale Green

Baxter Field in Sydenham (known as Baxters to the locals) is a grassy, open park alongside Sydenham School. The park is well-used by local people and nurtured by the Friends who work alongside Glendale, the company which 'delivers green space maintenance and management services to parks, sports pitches and community green spaces around the borough of Lewisham'.[30]

The Friends have planted spring bulbs and 400 saplings to create new hedging and soften the central playground, and regularly clear a little track through the trees and shrubs behind perimeter railings. A paved path runs round the top half of the park and is a useful jogging and cycling track, and the playground always seems to be filled with excited children.

The park is named after George Baxter (1804–1867) who was an engraver, printer and very skilled artist. In 1827 he married Mary Harrild, the daughter of Robert Harrild, a family friend, and settled in London. Robert Harrild encouraged Baxter to start printing and by 1835 Baxter had developed a new method of colour printing which was quick, efficient and much cheaper than existing methods. However, instead of becoming wealthy he ended his life as a bankrupt.

At some point the Baxters acquired land on Robert Harrild's estate in Sydenham where they built The Retreat, a large family house with gardens. The family used it as a weekend home but moved there permanently in 1860. Baxter was killed in a road accident in London and is buried at Christ Church Chapel in Forest Hill.

There is a small green off Kirkdale, with trees around three sides and railings separating it from a small car park on Peak Hill. The OS map of 1863 shows Peakhill Retreat just below Peakhill Road. The OS map of 1894–96 shows a large house called Leacroft in the same area, its parkland seems to correspond to today's Kirkdale Green. By 1894 this was Leahurst and I suggest George Baxter's home, The Retreat. George Baxter was a significant man in the history of colour printing and it would be good if this small green could also be enhanced in his memory.

Robert Harrild (1780–1853) developed a new way of printing and established Harrild and Sons, a company which lasted until 1958. In 1829 Robert Harrild rescued the upper part of the spire of the Church of St Antholin in Watling Street after a storm wrecked the building. (This was one of the churches rebuilt by Sir Christopher Wren after the Great Fire.) He paid £5 for the spire and erected it on his property at Round Hill Cottage. This spire, and the cedar tree, are all that remain of his home. Robert Harrild and his wife are buried in St Bartholomew's Churchyard.

Baxters is at Charlecote Grove SE26 4BW or Radlet Avenue SE26 4BZ. Kirkdale Green is accessed from Kirkdale Avenue or Peak Hill SE26 4QD
Opening times: Baxters 8 am to sunset; Kirkdale Green always open
Facilities: Children's play area, seats
Designation: Public park
Size: Baxters 1 hectare (2.5 acres); Kirkdale Green unknown
Friends of Baxter Field: www.facebook.com

Left: Joe taking a little break during a workday with the Friends!

Above: The Friends repainting the railings around the children's playground
Below: Equipment in the children's playground

Above: Alex, a young volunteer in the school holidays, sweeping up
Below: Kirkdale Green

Eliot Bank and Tarleton Gardens

The Earl of St Germans, and members of his family, were considerable landowners in Sydenham and south east London in the 19th century. Eliot was the family name and the origin of the name Eliot Bank which was thought to have been the boundary between Lewisham and Camberwell and also the boundary between the counties of Kent and Surrey in the past.

Eliot Bank is part of the hillside overlooking Dulwich and includes a residential development of town houses built in 1950s–60s. The hillside is part of a ridge of hills, 8kms long, which includes One Tree Hill in the north and stretches down to Selhurst beyond Crystal Palace. The ridge was quite a barrier to travelling out of London and when the railway line was developed it had to be sent through tunnels in the hills. The view over London from the hilltop is memorable.

The hills were once the site of the Great North Wood but Martin Knight suggests that while this was the site of a wood which was recorded hundreds of years ago much of the vegetation is from a later date. And while there may be trees which are several hundred years old these may not even be the original species because of the effect of evolution.

Eliot Bank is usually described as a hedge, but the strip of trees and dense undergrowth looks more like a miniature woodland. The trees include pedunculate and sessile oak trees, ash, wild cherry and holly trees and they are surrounded by indigenous undergrowth.

Tarleton Gardens is a private garden on the northern side of the 'hedge'. It includes some old oak trees, but there are mainly sycamores, lime trees, pine trees and old coppiced hazel. Large Victorian mansions, with equally large gardens were built here from the mid-19th century, and although some of the oak trees may be from earlier times the undergrowth includes shrubs found in gardens, including pear trees.

Access: Eliot Bank Lane SE23 3XE
Opening times: Eliot Bank Lane always open.
Tarleton Gardens closed to the public
Facilities: None
Designation: SINC of Local Importance
Size: 0.5 hectares (1.2 acres)

Eliot Bank in May

Hillcrest Estate Woodlands

The Nunhead to Crystal Palace High Level railway line was a branch line which was built to take visitors to the new Crystal Palace and which ran through the Hillcrest Woodlands. When the Crystal Palace burned down in 1936 the line was doomed and it closed in 1954. The London County Council bought the land in the same year and gave it to the local councils for housing and open space. Today a walk of 8kms called *From the Nun's Head to the Screaming Alice* traces the route of the former railway.

The booking office and station master's house at the former Upper Sydenham Station still stand on Wells Park Road and from here a path leads down on to the former tracks and a closed tunnel entrance. The sunken path through the woods emerges shortly at the housing estate of 1967 where a section of the Green Chain Walk leads up the hill, through more atmospheric woods, and out into Bluebell Close on Sydenham Hill Road.

Sydenham Hill was once in the Great North Wood and even today the hill offers hours of delightful woodland walking. In the Hillcrest Woods on Sydenham Hill you can find mature pedunculate and sessile oak trees, sweet chestnuts, ash and redwoods. Plants which indicate ancient woodland include wild garlic, native bluebells, sweet violet, dog's mercury and creeping soft grass. And there are indigenous plants which we could consider for shady corners in our own gardens such as pendulous sedge, broad buckler fern and red campion.

We are fortunate that local residents fight fiercely to protect what remains of the woods and prevent further building. This unlikely site is quite magical.

Access: Wells Park Road SE26 6RH and High Level Drive SE26 6XT
Opening times: Always open
Facilities: None
Designation: SINC of Borough Importance
Size: 7 hectares (17.3 acres)

Above: Former station master's house on Wells Park Road
Below: The closed railway tunnel through Sydenham Hill

The path down through the woods to the former railway line

Home Park

By the mid-1700s Home Park Farm was one of the largest estates in this part of Kent, but the value of the property and the desirability of the area were depressed when the Crystal Palace District Gas Company opened the gas works in Bell Green in 1858. At its peak the gasworks was one of the largest in the UK and employed over 2,000 people who needed to be housed, changing the social mix of the area. The Livesey Memorial Hall, named after Sir George Livesey, Chairman of the gas company, was built as a social club for employees and the war memorial at the Hall remembers employees and local people who died in WWI.

The last resident of Home Park Lodge died in 1896 and Lewisham Borough Council (then the Lewisham Board of Works) bought some of the land for a public recreation ground. The council also demolished Home Park Lodge and Home Park opened in June 1901.

A small public library stands on the edge of the park. It was one of the 660 libraries in the UK for which Andrew Carnegie paid. Albert Lewis Guy was the architect, Perry Brothers of Whitecross Street in the City built it for a total cost of £4,500 and the library opened in 1904. Mr Guy was a local man who practised for forty years from 195 High Street in Lewisham and also designed a library at Crofton Park, amongst other public buildings in south east London. The library was built on the site of stables attached to Sir George Groves' home. Sir George (of *Groves Dictionary of Music and Musicians* fame) was the first Secretary of the Crystal Palace Company and one of the key figures in Sydenham Society and he lived here from 1860 until his death in 1900. His grave is in Ladywell Cemetery.

Although Home Park in Sydenham is quite a small park it offers elegant open grassland and mature trees. There is a magnificent oak tree listed as Notable by the Woodland Trust and a similarly listed silver birch. The avenue of London plane trees, which was part of the original perimeter tree planting, glows in the autumn light and a sadly distorted old cedar of Lebanon stands near the roadside, probably damaged by pruning to allow buses and lorries to pass safely.

The play and exercise facilities are good and an interesting Adventure Playground is managed by Youth First, an organisation which aims to help the younger generation in appropriate and varied ways.

Home Park, on a busy main road, offers a calming open area with some magnificent trees.

Access: Sydenham Road and Winchfield Road SE26 5TH
Opening times: Always open
Facilities: Seats, children's play area, Adventure Playground
Designation: Public park
Size: 3.15 hectares (7.8 acres)
Friends of Home Park: www.facebook.com

Below: Pedunculate oak listed as a Notable oak tree by the Woodland Trust

The avenue of London plane trees in late autumn

Horniman Museum Gardens

John Horniman founded his tea company in 1826. He was the world's biggest tea trader during his lifetime and the first to sell packaged tea. But it was his son, Frederick John Horniman (1835–1906), who was the collector and whose passions resulted in the founding of the Surrey House Museum in his own home in Forest Hill.

The private museum opened in 1890 and was immediately very popular, and in 1895 the gardens opened as well. The collections continued to grow, forcing the family to move to another house, Surrey Mount, which stood at the top of the hill on the site of today's prehistoric garden. Eventually the collections outgrew the original building which was closed and demolished. Charles Harrison Townsend designed a new museum on the same site and it opened as the Horniman Museum in 1901. Frederick Horniman donated the new museum, its collections, and 15 acres of the grounds to the London County Council as a public museum. The conservatory (Grade II listed) was moved to London from the family home, Coombe Cliffe, in Croydon in 1986.

The original building is now listed Grade II* with further extensions added in 1912 and 2002. The museum specialises in anthropology, natural history and musical instruments. Frederick John Horniman was a serious collector, keen to develop public understanding, and the museum's continuing development has been guided by the seriousness and focus of F J Horniman's aims.

The beautiful gardens, listed Grade II, are also educational with particular concern for climate change and water conservation. There was a major redevelopment of the gardens in 2012 and the grounds offer a variety of different smaller gardens, and different habitats.
- A grasslands garden was designed by James Hitchmough and consists of North American prairie plants and South African plants. This complements the World Gallery in the museum and reminds us of climate change, demonstrating effective non-indigenous drought-tolerant plantings,
- The formal sunken garden dates from 1936, and has borders planted with a botanical collection of medicinal plants, dye plants and plants used to make items such as fabrics. The traditional planting of thousands of annuals is still continues but in the future this may be replaced by plantings which need less intensive management and are ecologically and environmentally more sympathetic.
- The bee garden is planted to attract bees and other pollinators. It has a sculpture which absorbs nitrogen dioxide pollution from the air (NO_2 prevents the bees from finding flowers) and insect hotels built from recycled materials.
- The prehistoric garden is planted with tree ferns, cycads, a monkey puzzle tree and a gingko. It includes a Wollemi pine, thought to be extinct until a specimen was found in 1994 in Australia. Today there are only c.100 adult specimens in the world. And of course there is a small dinosaur!
- The South Downs Meadow is hidden away on the eastern side of the site, and on the down slope of the hill. It is a perfect site for quietly contemplating the view.
- The Meadow Field is the open, grassed slope below the bandstand.
- Children (and adults) can play in the sound garden near the bandstand.
- The trees include horse chestnuts, dawn redwood, snake bark maple, ginkgo and a rare narrow-leaved ash tree.

This is a wonderful site in South East London: world-class museum, varied gardens, play areas, wide views, refreshments and a Sunday morning market — do not miss the Horniman Museum and its gardens, both of which will continue to evolve in the years ahead.

Access: Forest Hill SE23 3PQ
Opening times: Museum gardens open daylight hours, but please check website.
Facilities: Cafe, toilets, Nature Trail, tree guide, sundial trail, shop, Sunday morning market, butterfly house in the Horniman Museum grounds, miniature farm enclosure, and children's play area
Designation: Public park, SINC of Borough Importance
Size: 9.5 hectares (23.5 acres) including the Nature Trail
www.horniman.ac.uk

Sunday morning market at the Horniman Museum

Miscanthus in the Grasslands Garden

Fragrant roses in the Horniman Museum Gardens

Traditional planting in the formal garden

Horniman Nature Trail

The Nature Trail on the edge of the gardens is the oldest in London and opened in 1970. It follows the former High Level railway line between Nunhead and the (then) new Crystal Palace. The railway opened in 1864–65 but closed in 1954.

The trail is recent woodland with oaks, ash, silver birch, horse chestnuts and poplar trees and at the northern end there is a pond planted with grasses and flag iris, and a small meadow where wildflowers such as field scabious, wild carrot and black knapweed can be found.

In early summer the cow parsley flowers abundantly here, creating a magical walk through the trees. This little nature trail is a must-do!

Access: Forest Hill SE23 3PQ
Opening times: Museum gardens open daylight hours, but check website
Facilities: None
Designation: Public park, SINC of Borough Importance
www.horniman.ac.uk

Right: The Nature Trail leading to the pond and the green
Opposite: The pond at the far, northern end of the trail

Horniman's Triangle

Horniman's Triangle was converted to a public park in the 1950s but before that it was the smallholding of Sydenham Rise Cottage. The cottage stood in the upper, western corner of the site and there were chickens and geese in the field.

Today there are trees around the perimeter and a tangle of undergrowth where the ground rises up Sydenham Hill. An area of grass is left uncut and fills with clover, ragwort, buttercups and a profusion of small white daisies and flowering grass in the summer, with fruiting cherry trees around the edges.

Children always seem to be enjoying the play area under the watchful eyes of parents, and the park will no doubt become more popular when the new cafe opens!

Horniman's Triangle is a grassy expanse on the opposite side of the South Circular Road from the Horniman Museum, and not part of the Museum. This site is managed by Lewisham Borough Council.

Access: Sydenham Rise, Forest Hill SE23 3PQ
Opening times: 8 am to sunset
Facilities: Cafe, toilets, children's play area
Designation: Public park, SINC of Borough Importance

Below: Clover in the meadow in June

Below: Spider climbing frame in the play area

Children's play area in Horniman's Triangle

Mayow Park

In the 19th century there was increasing concern about working and living conditions in industrial towns, coupled with a belief that access to outdoor recreational spaces was beneficial to people's health, particularly the health of the working classes.

In 1829 J C Loudon published his pamphlet on *Breathing Spaces*, i.e. public parks; in 1833 the first Factory Act was passed to improve the working conditions for children and adults; and in 1840 a Parliamentary Committee under R A Slaney published a report on the *Health of Towns* which dealt mainly with housing and sanitation. But he was instrumental in the creation of the Select Committee on Public Walks which led to the Public Health Acts of 1848 and 1875 empowering local authorities to create parks and recreational spaces.

Steve Grindlay's writings on Sydenham and Forest Hill are always authoritative and he tells us that 'In May 1875 Rev Willliam Taylor Jones wrote *Plea for a People's Recreation Ground* which was published in the Sydenham, Forest Hill and Penge Gazette. He regretted that "all available land in our neighbourhood is being taken for building purposes" and young people "meet and loiter about the roads, congregate at every street corner, becoming a moral pest and a nuisance". Furthermore, the poor had nothing but "the streets, the music hall, the penny gaff or the public house for their evening's resort"'.[31]

At a public meeting in Sydenham in 1876 it was announced that Mayow Wynell Adams had offered 17.5 acres of his land at below market value for a recreation ground. The Mayow family were well-connected and attracted other major benefactors including F J Horniman, A G Hennell (the architect of the Forest Hill Library), T W Williams (the first Mayor of Lewisham), and the Rev William Taylor Jones who had campaigned so vigorously to establish the park. Lewisham Council agreed to establish a recreation ground in perpetuity — a park would only have been ornamental.

In June 1878 the Sydenham and Forest Hill Public Recreation Ground opened, the oldest public recreation ground in Lewisham. Around 11,000 people attending the opening, and a drinking fountain near the Brown and Green Cafe commemorates the festive occasion and the work of Rev William Taylor Jones.

The park is still well-equipped for exercise but also includes the Grow Mayow Community Garden and an orchard where eighteen heritage varieties of fruit trees were planted in 2012 with help from The Orchard Project.

The oak trees are the glory of this park. Mayow Park has the oldest and finest oak trees in the borough, second only to the oaks in Beckenham Place Park. Some trees mark the field boundaries from the time this was farmland; others have been previously pollarded, which is further evidence of farmland. The Woodland Trust lists seven Veteran, two Notable and one Ancient oak tree in the park, and at least one tree is estimated to be 350 years old. Other trees, such as the cedar of Lebanon, a monkey-puzzle, a magnificent holm oak, a tulip tree and black poplars date from the initial layout of the park and none are indigenous. (J C Loudon thought that c.700 new species of trees were introduced to the UK in the early 1800s.)[32] The Friends have produced a map of the park trees.

Come here just to admire and enjoy the trees and then having walked round, sit down and enjoy the fare at the Brown & Green Cafe.

Access: Mayow Road SE26 4JA
Opening times: 8 am to sunset
Facilities: Tennis courts, bowling green, soccer and cricket pitches, outdoor gym gear and trim trail, play areas for younger and older children, table tennis table, seats and picnic areas, Brown & Green Cafe
Designation: Green Flag Public Park, SINC of borough importance
Size: 7.1 hectares (17.5 acres)
Friends of Mayow Park: www.friendsofmayowpark.blogspot.com

Overleaf: Mayow Park in early spring

Mayow Park in June

One Tree Hill

One Tree Hill is in Camberwell but it is included in the book because it was originally in Forest Hill and part of the Great North Wood. This was the Oak of Honor Wood and legend says that Elizabeth I rested here on a visit to Lewisham. A nice story but perhaps not credible.

Because the hill is high (c.300 feet or c.90 metres) it was used for signalling. In the 1790s the East India Company had a semaphore station here which became a telegraph station during the Napoleonic wars (like Telegraph Hill), and there are the remains of an anti-Zeppelin gun emplacement during WWI. The Church of St Augustine, a Grade II listed building near the top of the hill, dates from 1873 and was designed by the aptly named William Oakley, to service the expanding community of the new Forest Hill district.

By 1896 most of the trees had been cut down and the hill was enclosed by the Honor Oak and Forest Hill Golf Club which rented the land from the owner, Alfred Stevens of Homestall Farm. After a campaign by local people Southwark Council bought the land for public use in 1905.

One Tree Hill is secondary woodland with ash, sycamore, wild cherry, hawthorn and blackthorn creating quite dense woodland which is controlled carefully to protect the old oak trees which marked field or parish boundaries. Unusually there are some mature London plane trees which probably date from the formal park at the beginning of the 20th century. And of course there is the 1905 Honor Oak, the third tree on the site.

Come here to walk, run, listen to the many species of birds or just sit and enjoy the view over London.

Access: Honor Oak Park SE23 1RA or Brenchley Gardens
Opening times: Always open
Facilities: Seats
Designation: SINC of Borough Importance, Grade 1
Size: 6.92 hectares (17 acres)
Friends of One Tree Hill: www.friendsofonetreehill.wordpress.com

Above: Enjoying the view from the top of One Tree Hill
Below: St Augustine's Church
Opposite: One of the mature oak trees

St Bartholomew's Churchyard

You can easily pass by St Bartholomew's Churchyard in Sydenham but do visit, and linger. As soon as you step inside the walls or pass through the lychgate you are in a quiet, somewhat derelict space but one which is also peaceful and calming, particularly in the spring. The churchyard walls so often create and protect a different level of being.

In 1824 William Dacres Adams wrote to the Bishop of Oxford, the Vicar's great uncle, and the Earl of Dartmouth, the Vicar's father, about the increasing population in Sydenham and their need for an independent church. Up to this point St Mary's Church in Lewisham was the parish church.

Eventually John Forster donated land and Lewis Vulliamy was commissioned as the architect. Building started in 1827 but the nature of the site required very deep foundations and increased the cost. Disputes continued, John Forster withdrew his offer, and the Church Building Commission was eventually persuaded to take on the project. The work was finally completed and the church consecrated in 1832.

There are several interesting graves around the church. A large tomb of 1853 commemorates Robert and Elizabeth Harrild and their family. Charles English, the first vicar of the new parish, who died on 31 May 1867, is buried in a colonnaded tomb. And William Dacres Adams is buried here, as are many of his family members. (He was private secretary to William Pitt the Younger when Pitt was prime minister.)

The yew at the entrance to the church guards the grave of ten men who died during the rebuilding of the Crystal Palace in Sydenham in 1853 when scaffolding collapsed. Their funeral at St Bartholomew's drew a large crowd. In 2003 the grave was restored, with a new information board, and was re-dedicated by the Bishop of Woolwich.

Camille Pissarro painted the church from Lawrie Avenue in 1871 and the view is similar today. A group of new fruit trees have been planted near the lychgate but a huge oak tree still spreads its branches over the graves at the front of the church and there is a fine larch tree near the south porch.

Access: 4 Westwood Hill SE26 6QR
Opening times: Churchyard is always open
Facilities: Seats
Designation: Church and Churchyard
St Bartholomew's Church: www.achurchnearyou.com/church/836/

Below: The tomb of Robert Harrild and his wife and the mass grave

St Bartholomew's Churchyard and the colonnaded tomb of Rev Charles English, the first vicar

Southend Park

Above: The upper level of Southend Park

Incredibly, Southend Park was still open countryside through which the River Pool meandered until after WWII, and it is only on the OS Map of 1961 that the park is enclosed by buildings.

The gate on Meadowview Road leads into the lower level of the park where there is a children's playground. Beautiful tall trees and densely planted shrubberies surround the grass and make this an attractive and secluded area. On the eastern side mature willow, alder and poplar trees mark the route of the River Pool. The river is hidden underground and only emerges on the far side of Meadowview Road where there is a very pretty walk along the river bank. Could the river be similarly opened up in the park?

A little bridge over the hidden river, and the remains of a cascade of water from the upper to the lower level divide the park into two levels. The upper level is more open, with varied trees around the central grass playing fields and attractive shrubberies around the perimeter. Shrubs include Mexican orange blossom, the beautyberry, elaeagnus, mahonia and berberis. There is some outdoor gym gear on one side and a small children's playing area in a far, shady corner. In the south east corner of the top level is an area which is managed as a closed-off wildlife area, like the similarly wild embankment above the houses on Meadowview Road. It is a curious landscape to find in an urban park.

Southend Park in south east London lies behind shops on Southend Lane and it could be truly magical if the River Pool is opened up again and the shrubs perhaps allowed to develop more naturally.

Access: Meadowview Road SE6 3NG
Opening times: 8 am to sunset
Facilities: Children's playground, seats
Designation: Public park, SINC of Local Importance
Size: 2.7 hectares (6.7 acres)

The lower level of the park in April with a small bridge over the former cascade

Sydenham Garden, Queensroad Nature Reserve and De Frene Market Garden

In the early 17th century the Worshipful Company of Leathersellers bought land in Lower Sydenham, including fields where Sydenham Garden, the Forest Hill Bowling Club and the Paxton Road estate are now situated. And in 1820–30 the Company sold the land to William Dacres Adam who married the daughter of Mayow Wynell Adams and through marriage inherited the Old House estate in Sydenham.

William Dacres Adam owned the 18th century Perry Vale Farm as part of the estate and today's nature reserve and Sydenham Garden seem to occupy the former orchard and kitchen gardens of the farm. The remains of greenhouses and cold frames were found here and the water pump, the only source of water for the farm buildings, still exists.

The farm buildings and their contents were auctioned off in 1831 and by 1851 the farmhouse had become a country mansion, Perrymount House. The house was demolished in 1937 and the grounds were gradually bought for new housing although the stables of the house remain at 14 Queenswood Road. In the 1980s Lewisham Council stepped in and insisted that the developer who had bought the remaining land sell part of it to the Council to create a small nature reserve which is now managed by Sydenham Garden.

The organisation was founded in 2002 and set up as a charity in 2004. It was extended in 2015 when the De Frene market garden was opened between the houses on Queenswood Road and De Frene Road on land that had previously been allotments.

The office building at Wynell Road has a green roof and organic vegetables are grown in raised beds next to a pond and alongside a beautiful new greenhouse. Hearsay has it that this was once a rose nursery; there was certainly a plant nursery in Wynell Road until the 1970s.

The Sydenham Garden and the De Frene Market Garden are Community Therapeutic Gardens which aim 'to promote the physical and mental wellbeing of residents living in South London by providing:
- a community garden where horticulture is used for therapy and rehabilitation
- opportunities for training for work and education
- opportunities for artistic and creative expression
- the protection and preservation of the environment for the benefit of the public through nature conservation or the promotion of biological diversity'.

Sydenham Garden offers Art and Craft sessions with an art therapist; Sow and Grow for people with early stages of dementia; Wellbeing Wanderers walking group; and gardening sessions. The Growing Lives project is based at the market garden and offers 'weekly social, therapeutic and vocational horticultural sessions, along with offering the chance to achieve Open College Network accreditation'.

The nature reserve is absolutely delightful in its urban setting and mostly woodland, with oak, ash, sycamore, hawthorn, blackthorn and elder. Perhaps some of the hedges were once field hedges? And could the old yew tree mark a field boundary?

The market garden is peaceful and beautiful, and a remarkable enterprise. Vegetables thrive alongside flowers, there is a small orchard, rescue chickens and beehives. On Open Days you may be able to buy some of the homemade honey.

If there is ever an Open Day you should grab the chance to visit these peaceful and secret sites.

Access to Sydenham Garden: Wynell Road SE23 2LW and De Frene Market Garden from De Frene Road SE26 4AB
Opening times: Open by appointment only
Facilities: Offices, seating, greenhouses
Designation: Nature reserve and Community Garden
Size: 0.29 hectares (0.7 acres)
www.sydenhamgarden.org

The greenhouse and growing garden at Sydenham Garden

Above: A seating area in the Queensroad Nature Reserve
Below: The pond at Sydenham Garden

Above: One of the greenhouses at De Frene Road
Below: Apples ripening

Above: Part of the growing area, greenhouses and sheds at De Frene Road
Below: Cornflowers, and a quiet corner under the trees at De Frene Road in June

Sydenham Wells Park

This elegant and calming park on the side of Sydenham Hill is a pleasure to visit all year round. Paths criss-cross the park and bring delights around every corner and it is a reminder of the genteel splendour of the area in the second half of the 19th century.

There are springs in the park and in the 1640s it was alleged that a woman had been cured of a serious disease by drinking the foul-tasting water. The word soon spread and twelve wells were opened up to cater for visitors, and to produce water which was also sold in London. This was not one of the fashionable wells, like Tunbridge Wells or Bath, but rather frequented by the 'common people'.

The popularity of the springs ended when the surrounding common was enclosed. Sir Francis Baring acquired the land which passed to John Forster of Southend in the 1830s. London was expanding and toward the end of the century T W Williams, the first Mayor of London, was concerned that all the land would be lost to building and led a campaign which resulted in the London County Council and the Lewisham Board of Works buying 7 hectares (18 acres) from H W Forster, John Forster's descendent, in 1898.

Lt Col J J Sexby planned the layout of the park which opened in 1901. There were broad paths, a water feature of three small lakes connected by a wandering stream with rustic bridges, a large pond, and a bandstand. Tennis courts, a boules pitch and a bowling green offered exercise opportunities. And by the 1930s visitors were talking of the beauty of the trees and the elegance of the park.

Today the artificial pond has been filled in to create a children's play area, and the boules pitch and bowling green have gone. In 1995 the gardens of two large Victorian houses on Longton Avenue were added to the park to create an area of woodland and a stone water feature powered by solar energy was erected in the sensory garden in 2007.

The trees are magnificent! There is one Veteran common hawthorn, but there are also old pedunculate oak trees, ash trees, beeches, limes, junipers, conifers and several dawn redwood trees. The springs still feed two ponds and a small stream, and willow trees bend over the water, with tall redwoods and oaks standing guard nearby. And around the two ponds are purple loosestrife, watercress, pendulous sedge, yellow flag irises and bulrushes. Moorhens, coots, mallards and Canada geese and even herons breed on the small island, enjoy the water and amuse passersby.

Access: Longton Avenue SE26 6QZ, Wells Park Road, and Taylor's Lane
Opening times: 8 am to sunset
Facilities: Playground for under-5s and older children, multipurpose ball court, outdoor gym gear, tennis courts
Designation: Public park, SINC of Local Importance
Size: 8 hectares (20 acres)
Friends of Sydenham Wells Park: www.sydenhamwellspark.org

Above: Alder tree leaves and fruit
Opposite: The pond in Sydenham Wells Park in May

Stately Conifers

Hornbeam

Copper Beech

Red Oak catkins

Sydenham Wells Park looking towards Crystal Palace

CROYDON CANAL AND RAILWAY LINE NATURE RESERVES

Canals were a popular form of transport for goods at the end of the 18th century and a network was developed around the country. The Croydon Canal, 15kms long (9.2 miles), opened on 22nd October 1809 and ran from the Grand Surrey Canal at the junction of Mercury Way with Surrey Canal Road in Deptford to a site which is roughly West Croydon station. The aim was to link the Thames with Croydon in the Surrey countryside and facilitate the transport of lime, timber, chalk and agricultural products.

Before the 18th century the area through which the canal was routed was farmland and centuries before that it had been part of the Great North Wood.

The canal followed the contour lines but needed twenty-eight locks to deal with the hills; sixteen of the locks were on the short stretch between Brockley and Honor Oak, and there were thirty-nine swing bridges and seven road bridges over the canal. The bridge at Eddystone Road was the site of Lock 22 swing bridge and the bridge at Dalrymple Road was the Brockley Swing Bridge. The Greyhound Inn in Sydenham was one of the refreshment stops along the way, as was The Dartmouth Arms, licensed in 1815.

Mayow Wynell Adams describes how he, his brothers and friends used to 'hire a boat at Doo's Wharf [opposite Sydenham Station] and row either to Croydon, or the other way to the first lock, halfway between Forest Hill and Brockley Railway Stations. Occasionally we had, in the summer evenings, a picnic in Penge Wood, boiling our kettle, gipsy-fashion, while listening to the nightingales'.[33]

The venture failed financially but the owners saw a business opportunity in the development of the railways and sold the land to the London and Croydon Railway Company. The Canal closed in 1836 and was filled in, and the railway from London Bridge to Croydon opened in June 1939, the second oldest line in London and mostly built along the line of the Canal.

The sites along the former Croydon Canal, and now the railway line from New Cross to Croydon, are Sites of Important for Nature Conservation of Metropolitan Importance, i.e. they are very important indeed and the wealth of trees, vegetation and birdlife was described in 2000[34] and by the Council in 2015. The sites are listed here from north to south.

Further reading:

Grindlay, Steve: *Croydon Canal Talk*: www.slideshare.net/foresthill/croydon-canal-talk
The Croydon Canal: www.canalmuseum.org.uk/history/croydon.htm

Opposite: St David's Road and the former Croydon Canal
Below: The Dartmouth Arms, one of the pubs on the former Croydon Canal

New Cross Gate Cutting

The New Cross Gate Cutting is also known as the Brockley Nature Reserve. The cutting is on both sides of the railway line but only the area on the western side is accessible. The London Wildlife Trust and British Rail signed an agreement in 1988 for the area to be managed as a nature reserve.

The area was open countryside or farmland when the canal was cut and still undeveloped when the railway cutting was dug out. It is thought the soil was used to make bricks and some of the brick spoil was returned to the embankments. There were brickfields close by, on the site of today's allotments off Vesta Road. And more Brickfields between Foxberry Road and Brockley Road (Brockley Lane in 1879), and at the junction of Wickham Road and Brockley Lane.

The nature reserve, like the others along the former Croydon Canal, is a very important wildlife site in London. It is mixed secondary woodland with sycamore, ash, holly, birch trees, a few pedunculate, Turkey and holm oaks, and tall, mature poplars on the top of the slope. A few grassy openings in the trees are filled with interesting wildflowers such as common toadflax, hoary mustard, oxtongue, and willowherb, and the brick fragments in the soil have created slightly acidic ground, encouraging varieties of grass to thrive. All of which encourages butterflies in the summer. Curiously there are also various non-indigenous plants such as buddleia (introduced from China c.1890), Michaelmas daisies, Virginia creeper and a plum tree.

Access: Vesta Road SE4 2NT
Opening times: Closed to the general public; check website for Open Days, generally once a month
Facilities: None
Designation: Nature Reserve, SINC of Metropolitan Importance
Size: 4.2 hectares (10.4 acres)
The site is managed by The London Wildlife Trust and Network Rail: www.wildlondon.org.uk

Above: Common toadflax
Below: A train in the deep cutting

New Cross Gate Cutting in early September

Buckthorne Road Nature Reserve

The Fourth Reserve was registered as a charity in 2019 with the aim of having the entire length of the railway cutting from New Cross to Forest Hill recognised as a statutory nature reserve, but progress is hindered because the land has multiple owners.

The charity has a particular interest in the Buckthorne Cutting which is in three sections: a privately owned section between Courtrai Road and the Eddystone Road Foot Bridge which has been designated as Ancient Woodland by Natural England and where there is a section of towpath; the middle section north of the Eddystone Road Foot Bridge, which is managed by the Fourth Reserve; and another privately owned section in the far north, abutting on the Dalrymple Road Bridge.

The Roman Road from London to Lewes followed the line of Brockley Way, over the railway bridge at the top of Eddystone Road, along a marked footpath leading off Eddystone Road, and on over Blythe Hill Fields. And although there are no signs of the Croydon Canal now, the Eddystone or Buckthorne Bridge and Courtrai Road line up with two swing bridges and locks over the former canal.

A curious feature of the site is septarian nodules, or rocks of compounded clay laid down millions of years ago when the earth was formed. They are associated with clay, which is common in London, and springs, but rarely appear on the surface of the ground, as in the Buckthorne Cutting. The railway cutting is very deep here and they were probably dug up when the line was laid down. The argument for springs is supported by a large reed bed in the northern, private part of the site, which also has a Notable willow tree.

The woodland is beautiful, with mature pedunculate oak trees and ash trees, and a single mature lime tree. Unusually there are also elm trees, and a coppiced field maple, and very old pleached hawthorns suggest hedgerows and field boundaries, which is of course the history of the area. A small signalman's garden is protected with a new living hedge, and horsetail is abundant alongside the bridge. This is another plant which thrives in wet soil.

To truly appreciate this site do visit on an Open Day!

Access: Eddystone Road SE4 2DB
Opening times: Check opening times on website
Designation: SINC of Metropolitan importance
Size: c.4.2 hectares (10.3 acres)
The Fourth Reserve: www.fourthreserve.org.uk

Above: Septarian nodules

The Raven's Nest at Buckthorne Road Nature Reserve

Garthorne Road Nature Reserve

Garthorne Road Nature Reserve lies on the eastern side of the railway line, opposite the Devonshire Road Nature Reserve. The land is owned by the railway company from which Lewisham Council obtained a licence in 1987 to manage the site as a nature reserve.

There are several small clearings in the nature reserve which are home to many varieties of grass and scrub. Restharrow, rosebay willowherb, ragwort and agrimony add colour. And bitter vetch, which is an unusual and rare plant in Lewisham, grows here.

The area was once part of the Great North Wood but it is secondary woodland now. The trees are mainly oak (pedunculate, sessile, and holm oaks), old hawthorn, birch, ash, hazel and holly, and there is a single coppiced lime tree. Wild clematis is abundant and honeysuckle is dotted about, plum trees produce fruit and blackthorn flowers in the spring. It is a beautiful site.

This reserve, unlike Buckthorne Road and Dacres Wood, is mainly undisturbed and this allows the flora to develop naturally, and encourages wildlife. Foxes, slowworms, birds and butterflies allow us to share their world, a small pocket of peace and balance, in our rushed urban life.

Access: Beadnell Road SE23 1AA
Opening times: Not open to the general public; check the website for Open Days
Facilities: None
Designation: Nature reserve, SINC of Metropolitan Importance
Size: c.2.6 hectares (6 acres)
Friends of Garthorne Road: www.garthorneroadnaturereserve.com

Above: Jersey tiger moth spotted in August
Below: Rosebay willowherb and ragwort in the grasslands

Ernie Thomason, Chairman, explaining the value of sycamore trees on the nature reserve with the railway line in the background

Devonshire Road Nature Reserve

Once upon a time this land was part of the Great North Wood; today it is secondary woodland which has re-established after the railway line was laid down.

Local residents were concerned that British Rail was cutting down trees and lobbied the council. Lewisham Council took up the cause and British Rail agreed to lease the site to the Council for an educational site which opened in 1981. The Devonshire Road Nature Reserve is in two parts: the area between the houses on Devonshire Road which was the site of a house bombed in WWII (the garden), and a stretch of land alongside the railway line from Honor Oak Park Station to Forest Hill Station.

The garden is well-established with fruit trees, planted borders which attract wildlife, a wildlife area to support moths and butterflies and three ponds. Local schools use the ponds for pond dipping and the garden has a healthy population of slowworms, frogs, newts, and toads. Indigenous plants include purple loosestrife, great willowherb and meadowsweet.

The railway land is quite different and quite magical with majestic oak trees, ash and sycamore, as well as hazel and hawthorn. Wander through the trees, past meadows filled with wild flowers in the summer, and enjoy the butterflies, the birds and perhaps even a fox. Everyday urban life just melts away.

Access: 170 Devonshire Road SE23 3SZ
Opening times: Open to the public on the last Sunday afternoon of each month
Facilities: One toilet
Designation: SINC of Metropolitan Importance
Size: 2.5 hectares (6 acres)
Devonshire Road Nature Reserve: www.devonshireroadnaturereserve.org

Top: Meadow Brown butterfly on ragwort in August

Middle: A slowworm in the garden

Bottom: Wild carrot

A path through the railway land area in Devonshire Road Nature Reserve

Albion Millennium Green

Albion Villas Road looks like a little country lane as it leads downwards to a small nature reserve which was created by local residents to celebrate the Millennium. It is protected as a registered charity and managed by volunteers with support from the Lewisham Borough Council.

The area has an interesting history because it was once on Sydenham Common and then one of two reservoirs for the Croydon Canal. The canal closed in 1836 and the reservoir must have been drained and filled in at the same time. Mayow Wynell Adams remembers that 'It was much used by the young men of the neighbourhood, myself among the number, for bathing in summer and skating in winter'.[34]

In 1847 Nos.3–6 Albion Villas Road were built by Robert Harrild, George Baxter's father-in-law. He was a wealthy man, thanks to his successful printing and manufacturing business, but he also speculated in housing and was the major developer of the Sydenham Park Estate, the area of the drained reservoir. In 1872 Miss Edith Elwes founded the Home and Infirmary for Sick Children and South London Dispensary for Women at nos. 5–6 Albion Villas Road. The Home was moved in 1885 to Champion House which stood at the junction of Sydenham Road and Champion Road, opposite Home Park, but was demolished in 1990.

In the late 19th century there was an orchard at the bottom of the road which was replaced with the Upper Sydenham Lawn Tennis Club until c.1985. The tennis courts eventually fell into disrepair and in 1998 the local residents decided to buy the site. They established a Community Trust under the umbrella of the Millennium Greens Scheme of the Countryside Agency and Millennium Commission, and in 2000 Albion Millennium Green opened to the public.

An orchard of twenty trees was planted in 2010, and a labyrinth was designed by local artist Maria Strutz in 2013. And everywhere pedunculate oaks, poplars, birches, ash, sycamore and hawthorn are growing up amidst the relentless buddleia and brambles.

This little green space will take you by surprise and you will want to have one in your own neighbourhood!

Access: Albion Villas Road E23 3HU and the path along the railway between Clyde Vale and Sydenham Park
Opening times: Always open
Facilities: None
Designation: Public open space
Size: 0.7 hectares (1.7 acres)
Friends of Albion Millennium Green: www.albionmillenniumgreen.online

Below: Bluebells in spring

Albion Millennium Green in December

Dacres Wood Nature Reserve

The Croydon Canal curved along the contours of the land but the railway line, on the contrary, could be laid out in a straighter line and this resulted in some curves of the canal being abandoned. The OS map of 1863–70 clearly shows an isolated curve of the canal in woodland, surrounded by fields on the site of today's Dacres Wood Nature Reserve.

By 1894 there were houses in the woodlands and the tree cover had been reduced, but the curve of canal was preserved in the garden of a house called Irongates. The London County Council (LCC) bought Irongates in 1962 and built Homefield House, but the garden, owned by the Greater London Council (GLC) from 1965, was ignored until it was bought by Lewisham Council in 1985 and the nature reserve opened four years later.

The matching and neighbouring house was Thriffwood which was demolished in 1952. Today a green space remains between the road and the fence of the nature reserve. Could this be the former garden of Thriffwood? And could it be added to the nature reserve?

The nature reserve is heavily wooded, with some mature Turkey oaks and horse chestnuts as well as pedunculate oaks, ash, lime and holly trees. A bridge divides the section of canal into two ponds which support a wide variety of invertebrates and which are used by schools for pond dipping.

This is another of the magical, hidden green spaces in Lewisham and it should not be missed.

Access: Honeyfield Mews SE23 2NH
Opening times: Not open to the general public; check website for Open Days
Facilities: None
Size: 2.4 hectares (6 acres)
Designation: Local Nature Reserve, SINC of Metropolitan Importance
Dacres Wood Nature Reserve: www.dacreswood.org.uk

Above: The outdoor classroom and kitchen in Dacres Wood Nature Reserve
Opposite: One of the ponds in the Dacres Wood Nature Reserve, a remnant of the Croydon Canal

Endnotes

1. Loudon, John Claudius: Breathing Spaces for the Metropolis, Gardeners Magazine, 1829, Vol V, pp.686–690. www.landscapearchitecture.org.uk
2. Dews, Nathan: *The History of Deptford in the Counties of Kent and Surrey*, 1884; FamLoc 2015, printed by Amazon, p.284
3. Loudon, John Claudius: *An Encyclopaedia of Gardening*, 1822, p.644, www.google.books.com
4. Sexby, Lt Col J J: *The Municipal Parks, Gardens, and Open Spaces of London*, 1905; reprinted by Scholar Select, p.123
5. Bishop, Peter, LDA Group, Director for Design, Development and Environment, 2010
6. Pevsner N and Cherry, B: *The Buildings of England, London 2, South*, Yale University Press, 1983, p.403
7. *The Diary of John Evelyn*, MacMillan and Co, 1908, pp.170, 229, 345
8. Sexby, Lt Col J J: *The Municipal Parks, Gardens, and Open Spaces of London*, p.130ff
9. Hart, F H: *The History of Lee and its Neighbourhood*, 1882; Leopold Classic Library, p.59
10. The Blackheath Society: www.blackheath.org
11. The Ecology Consultancy: *ReSurvey of the SINCS in Lewisham*, 2016, p.42
12. Loudon, John Claudius: *An Enclyclopedia of Gardening*, p.1231, para.2146; www.google.books.com
13. Browning, Paul: www.runner500.wordpress.com
14. Hart, F H: *The History of Lee and its Neighbourhood*, p.10
15. Hart, F H: *The History of Lee and its Neighbourhood*, p.9
16. The Ravensbourne Catchment Partnership: www.thames21.org.uk
17. Duncan, Leland L: *History of the Borough of Lewisham*, 1908; FamLoc 2015, p.v
18. Duncan, Leland L: *History of the Borough of Lewisham*, p.40
19. Dews, Nathan: *The History of Deptford in the Counties of Kent and Surrey*, p.281
20. Duncan, Leland L: *History of the Borough of Lewisham*, p.105
21. Browning, Paul: www.runner500.wordpress.com
22. Duncan, Leland L: *History of the Borough of Lewisham*, p.100
23. Duncan, Leland L: *History of the Borough of Lewisham*, p.96
24. Archer, John and Yarham, Ian: *Nature Conservation in Lewisham*, Ecology Handbook 30, London Ecology Unit, 2000
25. Friends of Beckenham Place park: www.beckenhamplaceparkfriends.org.uk
26. Leathersellers' Company: National Archives, GB 2158, Leathersellers: B. Estate Records, 4 (i)
27. Schüler, C J: *The Wood that Built London*, 2021
28. Thorne, James: *Handbook to the Environs of London,* 187; Godfrey Cave Associates, 1983, p.599
29. Besant, Sir Walter: *London South of The Thames*, 1912, Adam and Charles Black; Forgotten Books, p.295
30. Glendale: www.lewisham.glendalelocal.co.uk
31. Steve Grindlay: sydenhamforesthillhistory.blogspot.com/2008/11/origins-of-mayow-park.htm
32. Elborough, T: *Walk in the Park*, 2017, Penguin, p.79
33. Archer, John and Yarham, Ian: *Nature Conservation in Lewisham*, Ecology Handbook 30, London Ecology Unit, 2000
34. Adams, Mayow Wynell: *Sydenham, a Descriptive Account*, 1878; British Library, printed by Amazon, p.12

Sources

Books and articles, printed and online

Adams, Mayow Wynell: *Sydenham, a Descriptive Account*, British Library, printed by Amazon. (Original published 1878.) This little monograph gives a sympathetic insight into the development of Sydenham in the 19th century by one of the gentry.

Alcock, Joan F: *Sydenham and Forest Hill*, The History Press 2011 (Original published 2005)

Anderson, John Corbet: *The Great North Wood*, Forgotten Books (Original published 1898)

Archer, John and Yarham, Ian: *Nature Conservation in Lewisham*, Ecology Handbook 30, London Ecology Unit, 2000. The sites were re-assessed by The Ecology Consultancy, *Re-Survey of SINCS for Lewisham Borough Council*, 2016, and the report is online.

Barker, Felix: *Greenwich and Blackheath Past*, 1999, Historical Publications Ltd

Besant, Sir Walter: *London in the Nineteenth Century*, Forgotten Books (Original published 1909, Adam & Charles Black, London)
 — *London South of the Thames*, Forgotten Books (Original published 1912, Adam & Charles Black, London)

Butts, Robert: *Butts' Historical Guide to Lewisham, Ladywell, Lee, Blackheath and Eltham*, British Library, printed by Amazon. (Original published 1878.) A fascinating and early account of the area.

Clarke, William Spencer: *The Suburban Homes of London*, 1881; www.google.books.com

Collins, Lawrence Beale: *From First to Second Nature: A study of the River Ravensbourne in South East London*, UCL Department of Geography, 2010

Coulter, John: All John Coulter's books are carefully researched, with pertinent comments, and are essential reading about the Borough of Lewisham.
 — *Lewisham and Deptford in Old Photographs, a second selection*, 1992, Alan Sutton Publishing Ltd
 — *Lewisham History and Guide*, 1994, Alan Sutton Publishing Ltd
 — *Sydenham and Forest Hill Past*, 1999, Historical Publications, London
 — *Lewisham Past and Present*, 2001, Alan Sutton Publishing Ltd

Dews, Nathan: *The History of Deptford in the Counties of Kent and Surrey*, FamLoc 2015, printed by Amazon. (Original published 1884.) The book has short biographies of famous Deptford residents including Grinling Gibbon who was discovered by John Evelyn, and a list of ships built in the dockyards.

Domesday Book: Penguin Classics, 2003

Duncan, Leland L: *History of the Borough of Lewisham*, FamLoc 2015, and www.biodiversitylibrary.org/item/46090#page/78/mode/1up. (Original published 1908.) Leland Lewis Duncan was a Civil Servant and a Fellow of the Society of Antiquaries who lived in Lewisham.
 — *A History of Colfe's Grammar School, Lewisham, with a Life of its Founder*, 1910, printed for the Governors by The Worshipful Company of Leathersellers of the City of London

Elborough, Travis: *A Walk in the Park*, 2016, Penguin Random House

Environment Agency: 'A River Reborn — the Quaggy River', www.restorerivers.eu

Evelyn, John: *The Diary of John Evelyn*; MacMillan and Co, 1908
 Fumifugium, or The Inconvenience of The Aer and Smoake of London Dissipated, 1661, pp.1-47, Leopold Classic Library and www.google.books.com
 — *Sylva, or A Discourse of Forest Trees and the Propagation of Timber*, 1662; Amazon and www.gutenberg.org

Friends of Hilly Fields: *Birds of Hilly Fields*, 2020, Friends of Hilly Fields

Goodefellow, Liz: *London's burial grounds*, www.londongardenstrust.org

Grindlay, Steve at www.sydenhamforesthillhistory.blogspot.com
 — *Sydenham and Forest Hill Through Time*, 2014, Amberley Publishing

Hart, F H: *History of Lee and its Neighbourhood*, 1882, C North; Leopold Classic Library and www.books.google.com

Holmes, Isabella: *London Burial Grounds*, 1896; Amazon and www.gutenberg.org

Howard, Ebenezer: *To-Morrow, A Peaceful Path to Real Reform*, 1898; Cambridge University Press 2010

King, John: *Grove Park – its history revisited*, 2011, self-published
Lewis, C J Courtney: *George Baxter, His Life and Work, A Manual for Collectors*, 1908, Sampson Low, Marston & Company
Loudon, John Claudius: *The Villa Gardener*, 1850, London; www.google.books.com
    — *Breathing Spaces for the Metropolis*, Gardeners Magazine, Vol.V, 1829, pp.686-690; www.landscapearchitecture.org.uk
Lowe, J: *Former Water Works, Deals Gateway Deptford*, an archaeological desk-based assessment for St James Homes Ltd, November 1999; www.tvas.co.uk
Macartney, Sylvia, and West, John: *The Lewisham Silk Mills and the History of an Ancient Site*, 1982, Lewisham Local History Society
Mills, Dr Mary: Online articles for various publications: www.greenwichindustrialhistory.blogspot.com
    — *Greenwich Peninsula – Greenwich Marsh*, Amazon, 2020
O'Connor, Betty: *The Fight against the Theft of Sydenham Common and One Tree Hill*, 2008, www.thesparrowsnest.org.uk
Pevsner, N and Cherry, B: *The Buildings of England, London 2, South*, 1983, Yale University Press
Prockter, Adrian: *Forest Hill and Sydenham*, 1987, London Reference Books; www.knowyourlondon.com
Pullen, Doris E: *Forest Hill*, 1979, self-published. Fascinating stories by residents of Forest Hill, with listings of trades people and the graves previously at Christ Church Chapel.
Rhind, Neil: *The Heath*, 2002, Burlington Press, Cambridge
Rosewell, Roger: *The Mediaeval Monastery*, 2012, Shire Publications
Sayes Court — London's Lost Garden: www.londonslostgarden.wordpress.com
Schüler, C J: *The Wood that Built London*, 2021, Sandstone Press
Sexby, Lt Col J J: *The Municipal Parks, Gardens, and Open Spaces of London*, Scholar Select and www.archive.org (Original published 1905)
Slaney, R A: *Health of Towns*, 1840; Report of a Parliamentary Select Committee chaired by R A Slaney, www.archive.org
Smith, Godfrey: *Hither Green; The Forgotten Hamlet*, 1997, self-published, OOP
Spurgeon, Darrell:
    — *Discover Eltham and its Environs*, 1992,
    — *Discover Deptford and Lewisham*, 1997
    — *Discover Sydenham and Catford*, 1999, all three books published by Greenwich Guide-Books, London
    — *A History of Brockley in 10 and a half blog posts*: www.brockleycentral.blogspot.com
Steele, Jess: *Turning the Tide, The History of Everyday Deptford*, 1993, Deptford Forum Publishing Ltd
Thorne, James: *Handbook to the Environs of London*, Godfrey Cave Associates Ltd, 1983 (Original published 1876.)
Weinreb, Ben; Hibbert, Christopher; Keay, Julia; Keay, John:*The London Encyclopaedia*, 2008, Macmillan, London
Wood, Paul: *London is a Forest*, 2019, Quadrille Publishing Ltd

Websites
A Vision of Britain through Time is a website with historical maps and photographs: www.visionofbritain.org.uk/place/21418
Bertrand, Nick: Assessment of railway cutting nature reserves, www.fourthreserve.org.uk/background-1
Boughton, John: www.municipaldreams.wordpress.com
British History Online: www.british-history.ac.uk
Brown, M and Harris, C: www.croftonparkhistory.com
Browning, Paul: www.runner500.wordpress.com
Burials in Brockley and Ladywell Cemeteries: www.deceasedonlineblog.blogspot.com
Commonwealth War Graves Commission: www.cwgc.org
Community Gardens in Lewisham: www.lewishamgardens.webs.com
Darley, Kathryn: www.josephmyatt.weebly.com
Deptford Action Development Analysis: www.deptfordaction.org.uk
Edith's Streets: www.edithsstreets.blogspot.com
European Centre for River Restoration: www.ecrr.org
Forest Hill Society: www.foresthillsociety.com
Glendale Grounds Management: www.glendale-services.co.uk

Grove Park Neighbourhood Forum: www.grovepark.org.uk
Hidden London: www.hidden-london.com
Historic England: www.historicengland.org.uk
Howells, Jennie: *Bermondsey Street Back Stories*, July 2020: www.bermondseystreet.london
Ideal Homes: www.ideal-homes.org.uk
Martin Knight: Tarleton Wood: Is this the "real" Forest Hill?: www.martindknight.co.uk/7.html
Lee Manor Society: www.leemanorsociety.orgf
Lee Neighbourhood Development Plan: www.leeforum.org.uk
Lewisham Antiquarian Society Proceedings, 1902-07: www.archive.org
Lewisham Borough Council: www.lewisham.gov.uk
Lewisham Borough Photographs: www.boroughphotos.org
Nature Conservation Lewisham: www.natureconservationlewisham.co.uk
Ravensbourne Catchment Partnership: www.thames21.org.uk/catchment-partnerships/ravensbourne/
Ravensbourne River Valley, The London Landscape Framework, January 2011; Natural England Publications; www.publications.naturalengland.org.uk
Lewisham Green Spaces Forum www.lewishamparksforum.wordpress.com
Lewisham Local History Society: www.lewishamhistory.org.uk
London Burial Grounds: www.burial.magic-nation.co.uk/bgpage1.htm
London Gardens Trust: www.londongardenstrust.org The Inventory is an invaluable aid to exploring the green sites in London
London Wildlife Trust: www.wildlondon.org.uk/about

MAPS:
John Roque's map of 1769: www.southwark.gov.uk/council-and-democracy/maps-of-southwark
    Mapco: www.mapco.net/london.htm
    National Library of Scotland Ordnance Survey Maps: www.maps.nls.uk
Mayow Park Masterplan, 2009: www.aroundtheblockltd.co.uk/lib/file/4.pdf
Mummy's Gin Fund: A website with detailed descriptions of the facilities in parks, aimed at parents with young children: www.mummysginfund.co.uk/chinbrook-meadows/
Parks in London: www.goparks.london
Quaggy Waterways Action Group: www.qwag.org.uk
River Restoration Centre: www.therrc.co.uk
Sites of Geological Importance in Lewisham: www.londongeopartnership.org.uk
St John's Society: www.st-johns-soc.org
Street Trees for Living: www.streettreesforliving.org
Sydenham Garden Strategic Plan, 2019-2022: www.sydenhamgarden.org.uk
Sydenham Life Magazine: www.stbartschurchsydenham.org
Thames Water Archive: www.archive.thameswater.co.uk
The Baring Trust: www.thebaringtrust.com
The Brockley Society: www.brockleysociety.org.uk
The Hatcham Iron Works: www.georgeengland.org
The Open Spaces Society, previously The Commons Preservation Society: www.oss.org.uk
Victoria and George Crosses: www.vconline.org.uk
Walks in London: www.london-footprints.co.uk/walkslist.htm
Woodland Trust: www.woodlandtrust.org.uk The Woodland Trust has an Ancient Tree Inventory on its website

www.ingramcontent.com/pod-product-compliance
Lightning Source LLC
Chambersburg PA
CBHW041034020526
44115CB00035BA/3001